SCHOLASTIC

Teaching With Favorite
Ezra Jack Keats
Books

BY **PAMELA CHANKO**

NEW YORK • TORONTO • LONDON • AUCKLAND • SYDNEY
MEXICO CITY • NEW DELHI • HONG KONG • BUENOS AIRES

Teaching *Resources*

For Sasha and Eden,

the brightest lights

in the big city.

ACKNOWLEDGMENTS

Many thanks to Kama Einhorn and to Deborah Schecter for helping to shape this book.
Grateful thanks to the city of New York and to Ezra Jack Keats for helping to shape my childhood.

Jacket illustration from *The Snowy Day* by Ezra Jack Keats copyright © 1962 by Ezra Jack Keats, renewed 1990 by Martin Pope, Executor.
Used by permission of Viking Penguin, a division of Penguin Young Readers Group, a member of Penguin Group (USA) Inc. All rights reserved.

Jacket illustration from *Whistle for Willie* by Ezra Jack Keats copyright © 1964 by Ezra Jack Keats, renewed 1992 by Martin Pope, Executor.
Used by permission of Viking Penguin, a division of Penguin Young Readers Group, a member of Penguin Group (USA) Inc. All rights reserved.

Jacket illustration from *Peter's Chair* by Ezra Jack Keats copyright © 1967 by Ezra Jack Keats, renewed 1995 by Martin Pope, Executor.
Used by permission of Viking Penguin, a division of Penguin Young Readers Group, a member of Penguin Group (USA) Inc. All rights reserved.

Cover and interior design by Kathy Massaro
Interior art by James Graham Hale

ISBN: 0-439-60972-0

Contents

About This Book

*I*n his long and illustrious career as a children's author and artist, Ezra Jack Keats created a world that has enchanted readers for generations. Drawing from the simple experiences of childhood—from the wonder of exploring a snow-covered landscape in *The Snowy Day* to the arrival of a new baby in the family in *Peter's Chair* to the anticipation of a birthday party in *A Letter to Amy*—Keats's stories express the universal joys and trials of growing up. By creating a cast of lovable and three-dimensional multicultural characters, Keats ensured that readers from all backgrounds would find something with which to identify in his books. Having grown up in New York City, Keats drew on his own experiences to create the environment in which many of his stories are set. However, the children who populate this environment are representative of children everywhere. The result is a body of work that celebrates life in the city, but which also celebrates the experiences of children from communities all over the world. Keats created a neighborhood that every reader can recognize; it is a place in which every child can feel at home. In addition to his engaging characters, plots, and settings, Keats created a vibrant world ripe for exploration with his artwork. He is known for his use of collage, which adds a rich, tactile element to his illustrations. Young children learn about their world through touch, and they will find much to explore and discover in the pages of Keats's books. From the incorporation of fabric scraps to newspaper clippings, Keats's images tell a story all their own.

The activities in this book are designed to help you get the most out of Ezra Jack Keats's classic children's literature in your classroom. In addition to before and after reading discussion guides, you will find cross-curricular extensions in a variety of subject areas, including art, science, social studies, language arts, math, music, movement, and dramatic play. On pages 6 through 8, you will find general activities to use with Keats's books; on the pages following, you will find specific activities for 12 featured titles. For each book, you will find:

◎ **About the Book:** Book description and synopsis.

◎ **Concepts and Themes:** Central themes and concepts covered in the story.

◎ **Before and After Reading:** Discussion tips for enhancing children's literature experiences by tapping prior knowledge, making predictions, and relating the story to their own lives.

◎ **Extension Activities:** Suggestions for reinforcing and expanding children's learning across the curriculum.

◎ **Word Play:** Mini-lessons to help reinforce a specific literacy element in the text.

You will also find suggestions for culminating activities on the last page of this book; use these activities to wrap up your author study and celebrate all that children have learned. So invite children to take a trip into Ezra Jack Keats's neighborhood—a world in which all children are welcome to explore, learn, and grow.

About Ezra Jack Keats

Ezra Jack Keats was born on March 11, 1916, in Brooklyn, New York. Although he grew up in a time of financial hardship, Keats showed a strong interest in painting from an early age and found creative ways to express it. During the Depression, Keats's family had barely enough money to pay the rent for their crowded tenement apartment, let alone provide Ezra with expensive art materials. So, in the author's words, he "drew on and colored in everything that came across my path"—including the family's kitchen table. "I filled up the entire table with pictures of little cottages, curly smoke coming out of the chimneys…and kids." When Ezra's mother saw what he had done, she didn't scold him. Instead she said, "Did you do that? Isn't it wonderful!" Keats continued to grow as an artist throughout his school years, and in 1934 one of his paintings won first place in the National Scholastic Art Competition.

After graduating from high school in 1935, Keats was offered a scholarship to art school. But his family depended on him for financial support, so he went to work instead. He later joined the army and then spent some time abroad in France. When Keats returned to New York City, his career in children's publishing began. At first, Keats illustrated books written by other authors. He enjoyed his work, but felt that something was missing. "I never got a story about black people, black children," he said. "I decided that if I did a book of my own, my hero would be a black child." It was then that Keats found an old clipping from *Life* magazine in his studio; a picture of a small African-American boy from Georgia. Keats was drawn to the boy's face and expression—and the inspiration for Peter was born. Peter made his debut in *The Snowy Day*, which was published in 1962 and won the following year's Caldecott medal. Although Peter's ethnicity wasn't essential to this simple story, the use of a black protagonist was revolutionary at the time—and the book's success began a new era of multiculturalism in the world of children's publishing. Peter went on to appear in several more stories, and was joined by a cast of characters from a variety of cultures in more than 20 classic children's books written and illustrated by Keats.

The experience of growing up in New York City greatly influenced Keats's work: He never forgot the sights, smells, sounds, and sheer diversity of city life. He also drew on more personal experiences for his characters and plots: Peter's dog Willie is named after Keats's older brother, and the man in *Apt. 3* was actually his family's downstairs neighbor. But the real appeal of Keats's work lies in its universality: His stories are the stories of all children. Keats died in 1983, leaving behind a legacy of inclusion and a celebration of diversity that has changed the world of children's books forever. Ezra Jack Keats knew that the experience of childhood is one that is shared by people of all colors, shapes, and sizes, and he reflected that experience in glorious detail for all of his readers. As one young fan put it in a letter to the author, "We like you because you have the mind of a child."

Author photo courtesy of Penguin Putnam.

Exploring the Books of Ezra Jack Keats: Activities for Any Time

Many of Ezra Jack Keats's books are tied together by common threads: as children explore these books, they will become increasingly familiar with his beloved cast of characters and the neighborhoods in which they live. In addition to the activities suggested for each featured title, use the following activities to make connections between books and explore the author and artist's work as a whole.

Character Webs & Time Lines

Keats's work provides children with a unique opportunity to learn about the story element of character. As they meet the same children again and again in his books, readers get to know these characters intimately and watch them develop. Help children focus on character by creating webs and time lines.

- ◉ Have children begin a web for each character by drawing a picture in the center of a sheet of paper. Then, branching off from the center, have them write facts about the character. They can add new facts with each story they read. For example, a character web for Peter might be similar to the one shown at left.

- ◉ You can work as a class to create character time lines. After reading several stories featuring the same character, divide the class into small groups and assign each a different story. Have groups work together to draw a picture and write a short summary of what the character did in that story. Hang a string of yarn across a wall of the classroom and have children attach the pictures with clothespins, arranging them in an order that makes sense. For instance, Peter explores the snow as a very little boy in *The Snowy Day*; he is a bit older when he gets a baby sister in *Peter's Chair*; and he is even more grown-up at his birthday party in *A Letter to Amy*. Let children take turns looking at the time line and telling the events in the character's "history" in order.

Keats Family Tree & Story Graph

Keats created a "family" of characters who appear in different combinations throughout many of his stories. As children explore his work, they will meet Peter, his dog Willie, his sister Susie, their friends Archie, Amy, and Louie, and many more. Help children understand the connections between these characters by creating an ongoing graphic organizer. As children meet each character, write the name on a large index card and attach it to a bulletin board. Create a "web" of connections by attaching a string of yarn between characters' names and inviting children to tell the relationship. For instance, Peter and Susie are brother and sister; Susie and Louie are friends; Willie is connected to both Peter and Susie as the family dog. You might also create a graph to help children remember which characters appear in each story. Attach the titles across the top of a bulletin board and the names of the characters beneath each one. Invite children to recall what the characters did together in each story.

Story Sacks

Once children are familiar with Keats's characters, settings, and plots, invite them to mix them up to build new stories. Collect three paper bags, one for each story element. Write the names of several characters (*Peter, Susie, Amy, Archie, Louie, Roberto, Willie, the cat,* and so on) on note cards and place them in the first sack. Place settings (*Peter's apartment, Sam's building, Archie's stoop*) in the second sack. Use the third sack for plot situations, for instance: e*veryone goes to the pet show; someone is having a birthday party; the children build a magic spaceship.* Without peeking, have children choose two or more cards from the character bag, and one card each from the setting and plot bags. Invite them to create new stories using the information on the cards they chose. (For instance, Willie and the cat might chase each other around Sam's building and almost miss the pet show!) Invite children to write or dictate their new stories, draw pictures, or work in small groups to act them out.

Map the Neighborhood

City neighborhoods play an important role in many of Keats's stories. Provide children with paper and crayons and invite them to map where his characters live, including as many details from each story as possible. For instance, after reading *Apt. 3,* children might create a map of Sam's apartment building showing where each neighbor lives. After reading *A Letter to Amy,* children might map where Peter lives in relation to Amy and show the path he took to the mailbox. Encourage children to include shops, streetlights, sidewalks, and other urban details from the stories on their maps.

Collage Creations

Ezra Jack Keats used a combination of painting and collage for many of his illustrations. As you read the books, encourage children to point out any collage elements they see, such as wallpaper and fabric scraps, newspaper clippings, pictures from magazines, and so on. Add similar materials to your art center and encourage children to use them to add texture to their own paintings and drawings. Note that Keats used collage materials in a variety of ways, creating shapes with sharp edges by cutting, rough edges by tearing, and soft edges by painting over them. Invite children to try out each technique in their own work. Children might like to recreate Keats's neighborhood landscapes by painting city scenes and adding magazine clippings for elements such as billboards or street signs. They also might like to create a collage representing their own neighborhood. Display children's creations on a bulletin board and invite them to share how they used each material in their work.

Connections to the Language Arts Standards

The activities in this book are designed to support you in meeting the following standards outlined by the Mid-continent Research for Education and Learning (MCREL), an organization that collects and synthesizes national and state K–12 curriculum standards.

Uses the general skills and strategies of the reading process:

◆ Uses mental images based on pictures and print to aid in comprehension of text

◆ Uses meaning clues (for example, picture captions, title, cover, headings, story structure, story topic) to aid comprehension and make predictions about content (for example, action, events, character's behavior)

Uses the general skills and strategies of the writing process:

◆ Uses strategies to organize written work (for example, includes a beginning, middle, and ending; uses a sequence of events)

◆ Uses writing and other methods (for example, using letters or phonetically spelled words, telling, dictating, making lists) to describe familiar persons, places, objects, or experiences

◆ Writes in a variety of forms or genres (for example, picture books, friendly letters, stories, poems, information pieces, invitations, personal experience narratives, messages, responses to literature)

◆ Writes for different purposes (for example, to entertain, inform, learn, communicate ideas)

Uses listening and speaking strategies for different purposes:

◆ Makes contributions in class and group discussions (for example, reports on ideas and personal knowledge about a topic, initiates conversations, connects ideas and experiences with those of others)

◆ Asks and responds to questions (for example, about the meaning of a story, about the meaning of words or ideas)

◆ Follows rules of conversation and group discussion (for example, takes turns, raises hand to speak, stays on topic, focuses attention on speaker)

◆ Gives and responds to oral directions

◆ Recites and responds to familiar stories, poems, and rhymes with patterns (for example, relates information to own life; describes character, setting, plot)

Source: *Content Knowledge: A Compendium of Standards and Benchmarks for K–12 Education* (4th ed.). Mid-continent Research for Education and Learning, 2004.

The Snowy Day

(VIKING, 1962)

With this Caldecott Award–winning book, Ezra Jack Keats first introduced the character of Peter to the world. In his bright red snowsuit, Peter discovers the simple joys of a snowy day, from making tracks to sliding down an icy hill. Beautiful collage paintings and simple text express the universal, childlike wonder of waking up on a winter's morning to a world covered in white.

Before Reading

Invite children to share what they know about snow. Ask:

✳ In what season does it snow? Is it warm or cold outside?
✳ What does snow look like? How does it feel?

Show children the cover of the book and read the title aloud. Ask:

✳ What kinds of activities do you like to do on a snowy day?
✳ What is the little boy on the cover looking at? Who made the footprints?
✳ What else do you think the boy will do in the snow?

If you live in a warm climate, ask children if they have ever visited a place where it snowed. Invite them to share their experiences.

After Reading

Invite children to retell the story by describing some of Peter's snowy-day activities. Encourage them to relate the story to their own experiences by asking:

✳ Have you ever done any of the activities that Peter did in the story? Have you ever built a snowman or made snow angels? How did you do it?
✳ What is your favorite thing to make or do in the snow? What is something you've never done, but would like to try?

Next, draw children's attention to the part of the story in which Peter checks his pocket for the snowball he brought inside. Ask:

✳ Were you surprised that the snowball disappeared? Why or why not? What do you think happened to it?
✳ What can you see on the pocket of Peter's coat, where the snowball used to be? Why do you think there is a dark spot there now? What is it?

You might also like to discuss Peter's dream with children: What happened to the snow when the sun came out? Why was Peter so happy when he woke up from his dream?

Concepts and Themes

☼ weather
☼ winter
☼ snow
☼ changes in matter

Word Play

Revisit the story with children, inviting them to look for words beginning with *snow*. Words they might find include *snowsuit*, *snowball*, and *snowman*. Write the words on chart paper, using one color marker for *snow* and another color for the word ending. Invite children to look at the words and tell what they have in common. Explain that each is a *compound* word, or two words put together to make one. Invite children to suggest other compound words beginning with *snow* to add to the list, for instance: *snowflake*, *snowfall*, *snowstorm*, *snowboard*, *snowshoe*, *snowcap*, and so on. Children might also enjoy making up their own compound words, such as *snowpet* or *snowflower*.

My Snowy Day
(Language Arts and Art)

In the story, Peter wakes up one winter morning to find his world covered in snow. The book describes his adventures throughout the day, from morning to bedtime. Invite children to map out a plan for their own perfect snowy day.

1. Provide children with large sheets of drawing paper divided into three sections. Help children label the first section *Snowy Morning*, the middle section *Snowy Afternoon*, and the last section *Snowy Night*.

2. Next, encourage children to draw pictures of what they would do at each time of a snowy day. For instance, in the morning they might eat a bowl of hot oatmeal, in the afternoon they might make a snowman, and at night they might take a warm bath. Invite children to write or dictate a caption beneath each picture describing the activity.

3. You can post children's completed work on a bulletin board, or bind their pages together to make a class book of wintertime fun. Invite children to share their snowy-day plans with the group. Encourage them to tell why they chose each activity and explain their choice for the time of day.

Saving Snowballs (Science)

When Peter tried to save a piece of winter by placing a snowball in his pocket and taking it inside, he was disappointed to find that the snowball had later disappeared. Is it possible to save a snowball? Invite children to try an experiment to find out.

1. Talk with children about this part of the story, inviting them to tell what they think happened to Peter's snowball. Can they think of a way that he might have saved it? Invite children to brainstorm a list of places they might put a snowball to save for later. Ideas might include: on a shelf, in a refrigerator or freezer, outside, and so on. Write children's suggestions on chart paper as they dictate.

2. If possible, go outside with children and have them make real snowballs. Help them place each snowball in a self-sealing bag and seal it. (If no snow is available in your area, children can scoop crushed ice into plastic bags.)

3. Next, have children "save" their snowballs in the places they suggested. (Be sure that at least one snowball is placed in a freezer or outside on a very cold day.) When each snowball has been placed, invite children to look at their list again and predict which snowball will last the longest. Encourage children to explain their reasoning.

4. Check on your snowballs throughout the day and encourage children to watch for any changes. Which snowballs are getting smaller? Which seem to be staying the same size? Have any snowballs "disappeared" altogether? What is left in the bag?

5. Revisit the list, numbering the snowballs from "melted first" to "lasted longest." Discuss the characteristics of each snowball-saving place. Which was the coldest? Which was the warmest? How about lightest and darkest? How did these characteristics affect the melting speed?

Snow Fun Graph (Math)

Which winter activities would children enjoy most? Take a snowy survey to find out!

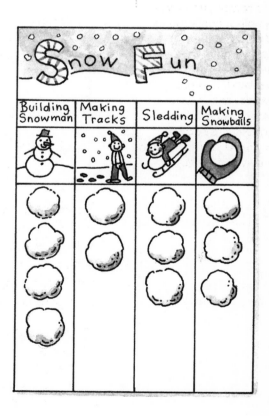

1. Look through the book with children to find the activities Peter did in the snow, such as making tracks, building a snowman, making snow angels, and sliding downhill. Write each activity across the top of a large sheet of tagboard. Invite children to suggest their own snowy activities to add to the graph, such as sledding or skiing.

2. Provide each child with a cotton ball and place a small dish of glue next to your graph. Invite children to come up to the graph, dip their cotton ball in the glue, and place it in the column beneath their favorite activity. If you live in a warm climate, invite children to imagine what their favorite activity might be.

3. When the graph is complete, discuss the results with children. Which activity has the most "snowballs"? Which has the least? Do more children prefer making snowmen or sledding?

Making Frost (Science)

Children can observe how frost forms right in the classroom.

◉ Fill an empty coffee can with ice cubes and add one-half cup of salt. Let children mix the ice and salt together with a spoon, then put on the lid. What do children think will happen to the outside of the can? In a few minutes, it will be covered with a layer of frost! Invite children to observe the frost crystals through a magnifier and describe what they see. Explain that frost forms when cold temperatures cause water vapor (gas formed from liquid) to freeze on a surface, such as the metal of a coffee can.

Snow-Person Glyph (Math and Language Arts)

Help children find out more about their classmates and practice reading symbols with a snow-person glyph. Make one copy of the reproducible activity on page 13 for each child (enlarge if possible). Provide children with scissors, glue, and crayons. Help children cut apart and then build their glyphs by giving them the following instructions as they work (children can also use the key as a reference):

◉ *Glue the pointy hat on your snow-person if you are a girl. Glue the round hat on your snow-person if you are a boy.*

◉ *Glue the plain scarf on your snow-person if you have one or more pets. Glue on the striped scarf if you don't have any pets.*

◉ *Glue square buttons on your snow-person's middle if your birthday is in the winter. Glue round buttons on if your birthday is not in the winter. If your birthday is this month, glue on the necktie.*

◉ *Glue mittens on your snow-person if you like winter. Glue on gloves if you do not like winter.*

◉ *Let your snow-person hold a broom. Glue the broom with the bristles pointing up if you like snow. Glue it with the bristles pointing down if you do not like snow.*

When children's snow-person glyphs are complete, invite them to decorate their work with crayons and write their name on the line. Display children's glyphs on an eye-level bulletin board and help them interpret each picture, using the key as a guide. What information can they find out about each child?

Variations: Use the snow-person glyph to represent different facts about children. Simply discard the preprinted key and create your own meaning for each symbol. You can also have children represent additional facts with crayons. For example, have children color their hat red if their favorite winter warm-up is hot chocolate, blue if they prefer soup, and green if something else.

Snow-Person Glyph

Name: _____

❄ Key ❄

= girl	= pets
= boy	= no pets

= winter birthday
= birthday not in winter
= birthday this month

= like winter	= don't like winter
= like snow	= don't like snow

EZRA JACK KEATS
WHISTLE FOR WILLIE

Whistle for Willie

◆

(VIKING, 1964)

(VIKING, 1964)

Concepts and Themes

▲▲▲▲▲▲

❋ pets, dogs

❋ exploring city neighborhoods

❋ persistence and accomplishment

Peter has a simple wish: to learn how to whistle for his dog, Willie. But try as he might, no sound comes out. After a day of practice around his city neighborhood (and other games along the way), Peter finally hears the wonderful sound that makes Willie come running. Children will cheer for Peter as they follow his path from hard work to success.

Before Reading

Show children the cover illustration and read the title of the book aloud. Ask:

❋ What is the boy doing? Who do you think Willie is?

Next, take a picture walk through the pages, inviting children to make predictions about the story. Guide the picture walk with comments and questions such as:

❋ Look at the boy's face in the beginning of the story. How do you think he feels?
❋ Do you think the boy and his dog live in the city or the country?
❋ From the last picture, how do you think the boy feels at the end of the story? Why do you think he feels that way?

Encourage children to describe the action on each page, telling what they think Peter is doing and making predictions about the story's plot.

After Reading

Invite children to reflect on Peter's actions and feelings by asking:

❋ Why did Peter want to learn how to whistle? How do you think he felt when he kept trying, but nothing happened?
❋ What other activities did Peter do around his neighborhood? Why do you think he kept going back to whistling?

Next, help children relate Peter's experiences to their own by asking:

❋ Have you ever tried to learn how to do something that was difficult at first, such as riding a bike or writing your name? What did you want to learn, and why was it important to you?
❋ What steps did you take to get to your goal? Did you practice a lot, like Peter did?
❋ Did you finally learn what you set out to? How did it make you feel? How do you think Peter felt when he finally heard the sound of his own whistle?

Practice Makes Perfect (Language Arts, Art, and Social Skills)

Learning something new can take a lot of practice—and a lot of patience. Invite children to show what they know with this activity.

1. Gather children together and brainstorm a list of skills that require practice to learn, such as playing a sport or an instrument, flying a kite, and so on.

2. Provide children with sheets of drawing paper and have them illustrate themselves doing an activity that they had to practice to learn to do well. Help children write a few sentences beneath their pictures, naming the skill and describing how they learned to do it. Encourage children to include any feelings they had during the learning process. Were they frustrated at first? Was it hard to be patient? Were they proud when they succeeded?

3. Bind children's pages together and create a cover. You might give the book a title such as "We Can Do It!" Add the completed book to your classroom library and read it often to celebrate children's achievements.

4. You might also like to invite each child to do an informal presentation of the skill he or she wrote about. Encourage children to demonstrate their skill to the group.

Make a Whistle (Science)

Experiment with sound and vibration by making simple whistles.

1. Provide children with plastic drinking straws and invite them to blow through the straws. Do they hear any sound? (The only sound children will hear is their breath moving through the straw.)

2. Next, help children flatten one end of the straw by pinching it between their fingers. Help them use scissors to make a small diagonal cut on each side of the straw's end, creating two V-shaped notches. Have children place the flattened end of the straw between their lips, placing their lips just past the notches. Then have them purse their lips tightly, take a deep breath, and blow as hard as they can through the straw. Do they hear a sound now? (It may take some practice before children can make a whistling noise. Encourage children to keep trying and be patient—just like Peter! You can also complete the experiment by demonstrating on your own whistle.)

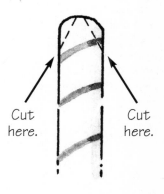

Cut here.   Cut here.

3. Once children have learned to make their straws whistle, experiment by creating whistles of different lengths. Cut the plain end of the straw off in varying increments. Does the whistle sound change as the straw gets shorter? Children will notice that the shorter the straw, the higher-pitched the whistle. You might explain that the notches cause the air in the straw to vibrate, creating the whistling noise. The longer the column of air, the lower the pitch of the whistle will be.

Word Play

Read the title of the story aloud to children. What repeated beginning sound do they hear? Point out the beginning consonants in the words *whistle* and *Willie*. Then help children look through the book for more words beginning in *w* and *wh*. Write a two-column list on chart paper as children find words. The lists might include:

whistle	Willie
whenever	wished
whirled	wink
why	way
when	went
where	walked

Read each list aloud with children. Can they hear any difference between the *w* words and the *wh* words? What sound do children think the *h* stands for? Explain that while the *h* is often unpronounced, or silent, these words can also be pronounced with a "blowing" sound—just like a whistle! Show children how to purse their lips and blow to make the *wh* sound. Then help them read the words again, this time differentiating between the initial sounds in each list.

City Clues, City Fun (Social Studies and Math)

Whistle for Willie, like many of Keats's stories, takes place in a city neighborhood. Help children recognize differences and similarities between city and country with this activity.

1. Page through the book with children, inviting them to point out any clues they see that indicate the story's urban setting. Things children might notice include sidewalks, streetlights, and the sides of big brick buildings. Next, invite children to imagine that the story took place in the country. What kinds of things might they see then? Ideas might include fields, trees, gardens, and so on.

2. Create a Venn diagram on a large sheet of tagboard, labeling one circle *City*, the other circle *Country*, and the intersection *Both*. Invite children to suggest items for each category, for instance: *tall buildings* in the *City* section, *farms* in the *Country* section, and *dogs* in the *Both* section. When the diagram is complete, encourage children to think about their own neighborhoods. Would they say they live in the city, the country, or somewhere in between?

3. Look through the story again with children, this time inviting them to point out ways children have fun in the city. Examples include sidewalk games such as jumping rope, drawing with chalk, and playing hide-and-seek. What are some ways to have fun in the country? Ideas might include apple-picking, hiking, or horseback riding. Create a second diagram to compare and contrast children's ideas. Point out that while city neighborhoods may be different from country neighborhoods, they can both be wonderful places to live.

Make an Accordion Book (Language Arts and Art)

Help children practice sequencing skills and story structure with a book that is fun to make and read. Willie the dachshund's long body is the perfect shape for an accordion book! Make one copy of page 18 for each child (enlarge if possible), and help children create the books as follows:

1. Help children cut on the dashed lines to make two strips: one for the dachshund's front and one for its back. Next, help them tape the strips together to make one long dachshund.

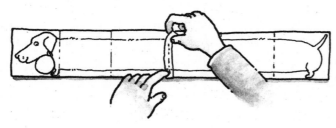

2. Invite children to think of a story they would like to tell. Children can recreate the story line of *Whistle for Willie*, or they can write their own story about what they would do if Willie was their pet. Have children write or dictate what happens first, next, then, and last on each section of the book. Encourage them to create illustrations to go with their text. Have children write the title of their story on Willie's tag.

3. When children have finished, show them how to fold the book's sections on the lines, accordion style. (See below.) They can then pull Willie's head and tail apart to read the story inside. Invite children to share their books with the group, trade them with friends, or bring them home to read with their families.

Additional Resources

The Little French Whistle
by Carole Lexa Schaefer
(Knopf, 2002)

Children will enjoy "whistling along" to this onomatopoetic tale about Louie's brand-new whistle and the sounds it can make.

Pretzel
by Margret Rey
(Houghton Mifflin, 1997)

First published in 1944, this book by one of the creators of *Curious George* tells the story of Pretzel, a dachshund puppy who grows—and grows—to be the longest dog in the world.

Whistling
by Elizabeth Partridge
(HarperCollins, 2001)

Beautiful quilt illustrations enhance this story of a small boy who goes on an overnight camping trip with his father—and learns how to whistle just the right note to wake up the sun.

Willie's Birthday
by Anastasia Suen
(Viking, 2001)

This book is part of the Peter's Neighborhood series, a collection of early readers featuring Keats's beloved characters. Children will enjoy following the continued adventures of Peter and Willie, and seeing what happens as the dachshund's birthday party gets out of hand!

Make an Accordion Book

Next, _____
_____ .

First, _____
_____ .

by _____
_____ .

Last, _____
_____ .

Then, _____
_____ .

Teaching With Favorite Ezra Jack Keats Books   Scholastic Teaching Resources

Peter's Chair

❖❖

(H A R P E R   &   R O W ,   1 9 6 7)

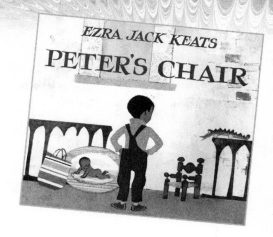

Everything has changed for Peter since the new baby arrived. His parents have given his sister his old cradle and crib—and they've painted them pink! But when Peter decides to save his baby chair for himself, he makes an important discovery: he has grown too big for it. Children are sure to relate to Peter's dilemma in this classic story about families, siblings, and growing up.

Concepts and Themes

▲▲▲▲▲▲

☼ **siblings, families**

☼ **growing and changing**

☼ **giving and sharing**

Before Reading

Invite children to share what they know about families. What is a family? How many family members do they live with? Do they have any brothers or sisters? Are they younger or older? Ask children if anyone has experienced the arrival of a new baby in the family. Encourage them to share their experiences by asking questions such as the following:

✳ How did you feel when you found out you were getting a baby brother or sister? Were you excited?

✳ What happened when the baby was born? What was different or new for you?

✳ Did you help take care of the baby? What kinds of things did you do?

After Reading

Talk with children about Peter's experiences in the story. Why do children think Peter was upset to have his old furniture painted and given to his sister? Have they ever had to pass down clothing or toys to a younger sibling, or have they had hand-me-downs given to them? Next, invite children to connect to Peter's feelings about his chair. Ask:

✳ Why didn't Peter want Susie to have his chair? What made him change his mind?

✳ Were you surprised to see that Peter had grown too big for the chair? Why or why not?

When children have had a chance to respond, invite them to think about themselves as babies. Ask:

✳ How are you different now from when you were a baby?

✳ What things can you do now that you couldn't do then?

The Sharing Chair (Social Skills)

In the story, Peter has a special chair that he has trouble sharing with his new sister. Why not create a special chair in your classroom for children to share?

1. Designate a "sharing chair" and place it in a central location of the classroom, such as the circle-time rug or other gathering place.

2. Invite children to decorate the chair by tying on ribbons or yarn, or adding streamers. (If the chair is school property, be sure to use only removable adhesive to attach the decorations.) Create a laminated sign reading "_____'s Chair" and attach it to the chair back.

3. Each day or each week, write a child's name on the blank using a water-based marker. Invite the child to sit in his or her special chair and share things with the group, such as stories, artwork, or show-and-tell items.

4. On a rotating basis, wipe off the sign and write a new child's name on the blank. This is a surefire way to make children feel special, as well as helping them learn to share the "spotlight."

Family Graph (Math and Social Studies)

Reinforce the concept that all families are different by creating a family graph.

1. Write children's names in a vertical column along the left side of a sheet of chart paper or tagboard.

2. Create small and large "paper doll" templates—you might use two sizes of gingerbread man cookie cutters. Invite children to use the templates to cut people shapes out of colored construction paper. Be sure to use two different colors of paper, for instance, red and yellow.

3. Once you have a supply of large and small "people," invite children up to the chart to graph the family members that live with them. Have them use the large size to represent adults and the small size to represent children. Designate one color for males and one for females.

4. When the graph is complete, discuss the results with children. Help them read the symbols to figure out the makeup of each child's family. Be sure to emphasize to children that a family is a group of people who love and care for one another—large or small, all families are special.

Guess Who? Bulletin Board (Science)

Reinforce the concepts of
growth and change with a
lift-the-flap bulletin board.

1. In advance, invite family
members to send in two
photographs of their
child: one baby photo
and one current photo.

2. Attach each photo to a sheet of construction paper and staple the sheets
together across the top edge, with the baby photos on top. Then attach
all the sheets to a bulletin board at children's eye level.

3. Invite children to look at each baby picture, guess who it is, and then lift
the flap to find out! Use the bulletin board as a springboard for discussion
about how children have grown and changed since they were babies.

Family Tree Portraits (Art)

Try a twist on a family portrait
activity by inviting children to create
family trees.

1. Have children draw a tree shape
on a sheet of plain paper.

2. Next, help children cut leaf
shapes out of light-colored
construction paper. Then have
them draw the members of their
family on the leaf shapes, using
one leaf for each family member.

3. Invite children to glue a leaf to
each branch to create a family
tree. Explain that the oldest
members of the family should be
placed on the highest branches, and the youngest members on the lowest
branches. You might help children label the leaves with each family
member's name.

4. Display children's family trees on a wall of the classroom for display and
discussion.

Word Play

Revisit the title of the
story with children.
Read the phrase *Peter's
Chair* aloud, drawing
children's attention to the
apostrophe. What do
children think this symbol
means? Explain that an
apostrophe followed by
an *s* after someone's
name often indicates a
possessive—in this case,
it means that the chair
belongs to Peter. Page
through the book with
children to find other
examples of possessives
(*Susie's room, sister's
high chair*).

Invite children to
practice using the
structure with their own
names as they point to
objects that belong to
them (*Alice's coat, Carlo's
book*, and so on). Write
children's possessive
phrases on chart paper.
Children might like to
create labels on sticky
notes to attach to their
items, using the chart
as a reference.

Taking Care of Baby (Social Studies and Dramatic Play)

Having a new baby in the family can be very exciting—and very hard work!

◎ Invite children with younger siblings (or other relatives) to share their experiences with babies. What do babies need? What are some ways to help take care of a baby? If possible, invite family members with babies or very young children to visit the classroom for an interview. Ask them to talk with children about what babies eat, when they are fed, when they sleep, and so on. Children might also enjoy hearing their parents or caregivers tell what they themselves were like when they were babies! What was their favorite food? What were their first words? Invite children to "practice" taking care of babies in the dramatic play center. Children with younger siblings might like to "teach" their classmates the caregiving skills they have learned.

"How I've Grown" Minibook (Language Arts)

Have children make their own minibooks showing how they have grown.

◎ Use two blank pieces of white paper, fold them in half to form a book, and staple at the binding. On the cover, they can write "How I've Grown." On page 1, invite them to draw a picture of themselves as they looked when they were babies and label it "Here's me when I was a baby." On page 2, invite children to draw a picture of themselves as they look now and label it "Here's me now." Then, for pages 3–4 and 5–6, encourage children to think of something that they do differently now from when they were babies. Help them complete the sentences: "When I was a baby, I _____. Now I can _____." Children can draw pictures illustrating their sentences. You might invite children to share their books with the group at circle time.

A Letter to Amy

(HARPER & ROW, 1968)

Peter is inviting only one girl to his birthday party: his friend Amy. Rather than asking her in person, he decides to send her a special invitation—but a thunderstorm on the way to the mailbox sends Peter's plans into a tailspin. Will Amy get the letter in time? And will she come to Peter's party? This story's themes of communication and friendship are sure to resonate with boys and girls alike.

Before Reading

Begin a discussion with children about letters and mail. Have children ever sent or received a letter? Ask:

✳ Would you rather get a letter in the mail from a special friend, or talk to them on the phone? How would you feel if you went home today and found a letter addressed to you in your mailbox?

✳ What kinds of things do people tell each other in letters? If you were to write a letter, who would you write to and what would you say?

Next, show children the cover of the book and read the title aloud. Invite children to make predictions about the story by asking:

✳ What do you think the letter to Amy is about? What might the boy want to say?

✳ What is the weather like? What do you think will happen to the letter?

After Reading

Talk with children about the characters' feelings throughout the story. Ask:

✳ Why do you think Peter wanted to send a special invitation to Amy?

✳ Why didn't Peter want Amy to see the letter? How did Amy feel when he bumped into her and grabbed the letter?

✳ How did Peter feel when he finally saw Amy at his party?

Next, discuss the weather in the story and how it affected the characters and plot. Ask:

✳ Why did Peter have so much trouble mailing the letter? How do you think he felt on the way home from the mailbox? How do you feel on rainy days?

Invite children to talk about any birthday parties they may have had. Did they invite any friends? Did they send out invitations or ask their friends in person? Which way do children think is better, and why?

Concepts and Themes

▲ ▲ ▲ ▲ ▲ ▲

☼ letters, mail

☼ weather: rain, wind

☼ birthdays

☼ friendship

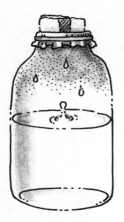

Rain in a Jar (Science)

Rain is an important element in *A Letter to Amy*. Children can find out how rain works by making their own rainfall.

1. Gather several large, clear jars or bowls, sheets of plastic wrap, and several ice cubes. Fill each jar with hot water, supervising closely for safety. Help children cover the top tightly with plastic wrap. Put a few ice cubes on top.

2. Encourage children to watch closely to see what will happen inside the jar. Soon they will see a "cloud" forming under the plastic and "raindrops" beginning to fall back into the water! This is because some of the hot water has evaporated and turned into water vapor. When the vapor hits the cold plastic, it condenses into drops which fall back into the water. Children have just witnessed the water cycle right in the classroom.

Watching the Wind (Science and Art)

In the story, a windy day caused Peter a lot of trouble. Children can have fun exploring the properties of wind with a project that combines art and science.

1. To make wind socks, provide each child with half of an empty paper towel tube and colored tissue or crepe paper cut into 1/4-inch by 6-inch strips. First, let children decorate the outside of the tube with crayons, markers, or paints.

2. Next, have children smear glue along the inner edge of one end of the tube. Then have them attach the ends of several tissue paper strips to the inside of the tube. (The strips should be placed close together and can even overlap a bit.)

3. Help children punch three holes at equal points in the opposite end of the tube. Provide each child with two 6-inch lengths of yarn and one 12-inch length of yarn. Thread each piece of yarn through a hole and tie the ends in place. Then tie all three pieces together to complete the wind sock.

4. You can begin your wind explorations indoors with an electric fan. Start by turning the fan on at its lowest setting. Let children take turns holding their wind socks in front of the fan (with the tails facing away from the fan). What happens to the tissue strips? Invite children to predict what will happen when the fan is turned higher, then try it to find out. (If you have an oscillating fan, you can also experiment with wind direction.)

5. Invite children to use the wind socks outdoors on the next breezy day. Have them hold their sock by the long length of yarn and watch as the tail flies behind them like a kite. Children can also experiment by running at different speeds with their socks in hand. This is a colorful way to watch wind at work!

It's Party Time! (Language Arts and Social Skills)

In the story, Peter's mother helps him include the right information on his invitation to Amy. Why not help children practice invitation-writing by having your own celebration?

◎ Have a party for an upcoming birthday, a special event, or simply to celebrate friendship and sharing. You can invite another classroom to join you. Encourage children to tell what information they think is important to include in their announcements (they might like to look in the book for reference). Then help children create invitations that include the date, time, place, and theme of your party. (The postcard pattern on page 27 can double as an invitation. Have children write the party information on the left and a child's name and classroom number on the right. Children can draw party symbols such as hats and streamers on the front of the card.) Help children deliver their completed invitations. On the day of the party, encourage children to thank their guests for coming to join in the fun.

Birthday Wish Graph (Math)

When it's time for birthday cake, Peter's friends suggest several wishes for him to make—but Peter makes his own wish before he blows the candles out. Revisit this part of the story and use it as a springboard for a fun graphing activity.

1. Discuss the end of the story with children. What do they think Peter wished for? What kinds of wishes have they made on their own birthdays? Write children's ideas on a sheet of chart paper.

2. Create several "cakes" from large rectangles of tagboard and let children decorate. Create "candles" from strips of colored construction paper. Give each child a candle and have children label them with their names.

3. Next, choose several wishes from the list children created earlier. Write each one on a large sticky note and attach the wishes to the cake shapes. Help children read each wish. They can attach their candle to the cake with their favorite wish using removable adhesive.

4. When all the candles have been placed, help children count the candles on each cake and interpret the results. Which wish was the most popular? Which was the least popular? Try the activity again, using different wishes from the list.

Look through the book with children for words related to weather. Words they might find include: *rain, clouds, lightning, thunder,* and *wind.* Write these words on index cards and attach them to a bulletin board to begin a weather word wall. Invite children to suggest additional nouns and descriptive words for the wall, such as *snow, storm, sunny, warm, cold,* and so on. Encourage children to observe the weather each day and record it on your classroom calendar using a word from the wall. If children cannot find a word to match the day's weather, it is time to add a new one to your collection!

Additional Resources

Dear Juno
by Soyung Pak
(Viking, 1999)

When Juno cannot read the letter he receives from his Korean grandmother, he discovers a way to send messages in a language both of them can understand.

Dear Mr. Blueberry
by Simon James
(Margaret K. McElderry, 1991)

This delightful story unfolds in epistolary form, as a little girl discovers a whale in her pond and writes to her teacher asking just what she should do about it.

Dear Mrs. LaRue: Letters From Obedience School
by Mark Teague
(Scholastic, 2002)

This humorous take on letter-writing features a clever dog who tirelessly writes to his owner to spring him from obedience school.

The Jolly Postman or Other People's Letters
by Janet & Allan Ahlberg
(Little Brown & Co., 1986)

As this fairytale postman delivers mail to familiar friends such as the Three Bears, children can pull each actual letter from its envelope and see it for themselves!

Postcard to a Pal (Language Arts and Art)

Invite children to send messages to special friends by creating a post office right in the classroom.

1. In advance, collect a shoebox for each child in the class. Invite children to decorate their shoebox with paints or collage materials, and help them cut a slit in the lid. Assign each child a different number and have children write their name and number on the box to create an "address."

2. Make one copy of page 27 for each child. Help children cut out the postcard, fold in the middle, and seal using a glue stick. Then assign each child a secret "Postcard Pal." Have children write the pal's name and "address" and include a message. Children might like to write about what makes their pal a good friend. Then have them flip the postcard over and draw a picture of how they like to spend time with their pal.

3. Encourage children to deliver their mail by matching the name and number on the postcard to the correct mailbox address. When all the postcards have been delivered, let children open their mailboxes to find their Postcard Pal's message. You might like to keep a supply of postcards in your writing center so children can send one another messages throughout the year.

Variation: You can also try sending the postcards through the real postal service. Be sure to copy the postcards onto heavy paper for durability, and have children seal the front and back together well. Children can design and send postcards to friends, relatives, or even to family members at their own address—and then watch to see when it arrives! (Note that the postcard is not regulation size and therefore will require a letter-rate stamp.)

Postcard to a Pal

Postcard Back

Dear ____________________,

____

____

____

____

____

____

From ____________________

To:

____

____

____

Fold

Postcard Front

Hi, Cat!

❖❖

(MACMILLAN, 1970)

Peter's friend Archie loves to entertain the neighborhood children with his funny impressions and performances. But when Archie says "Hi" to the stray cat on his block, he finds that he has a new admirer—and that cat seems determined to take center stage! After a day of mishaps and frustration with his unwanted companion, Archie discovers that his new feline friend makes him feel special.

Concepts and Themes

▲▲▲▲▲▲

✳ stray animals

✳ animal friends, cats

✳ performing

✳ imagination and make-believe

Before Reading

Invite children to share any experiences they may have had with stray cats, dogs, or other animals. Ask:

✳ Have you ever seen an animal in your neighborhood who was lost, or who didn't seem to have a home? Have you ever had a stray animal follow you home or come to your door? What happened next?

✳ What could you do to help a stray cat or dog?

As children share their ideas, be sure to point out important safety tips for dealing with stray animals. Then show children the cover of the book and invite them to make predictions about the story. Ask:

✳ Do you think the boy and the cat will become friends?

✳ Do you think animals can make good friends for people? Why or why not?

After Reading

Invite children to retell key parts of the story and share their thoughts. Ask:

✳ How do you think Archie felt about the cat when he first saw it? How did he feel when the cat interrupted his show?

✳ Did Archie's feelings about the cat change by the end? Why do you think so?

✳ Why do you think the cat followed Archie around?

Turn to the last page of the story and read the ending aloud once more. Ask:

✳ Who is sitting outside Archie's door while he tells his mother about his adventures? Does Archie know that the cat followed him? What do you think will happen next?

Encourage children to use their imaginations to extend the story. If they were Archie, would they try to find the cat's owner? Would they like to adopt the cat as their own pet? What adventures might they have with the cat?

Animal Friend Treats (Social Studies and Cooking)

Help the homeless cats and dogs in your area by making a donation to a local animal shelter. Children will enjoy baking treats for their animal friends, and feel pride in making a contribution to their community. Use the following recipe to make biscuits that will be appreciated by felines and canines alike.

When the biscuits have cooled, store them in a tin and tie with ribbons. Children might also like to create a card to wish the animals luck in finding good homes, as well as to thank the shelter workers for taking good care of their animal friends. Deliver your donation to the shelter and make a difference in an animal's day!

Animal Friend Treats

2 cups whole wheat flour

1/2 cup cornmeal

2/3 cup water

6 tablespoons oil

1. Measure all the ingredients into a large bowl. Mix well.
2. Roll out the dough to 1/4 inch thickness.
3. Use cookie cutters to cut the dough into shapes.
4. Bake on a cookie sheet at 350° for 35–40 minutes.

Mr. Big Face Parade (Art)

When Archie uses a paper bag to become "Mr. Big Face," the neighborhood children are delighted. Invite children to create their own versions of "Mr. Big Face" and have a parade.

1. Provide each child with a large paper grocery bag, scissors, paints, crayons, markers, and collage materials such as fabric scraps, yarn, glitter, and so on. Help children create neck and arm holes by cutting circles out of the bottom and sides of the bag.

2. Next, invite children to create a paper-bag character using the decorative materials. They can paint a face on the front of the bag, and use collage materials such as yarn for hair or glitter for a necklace. Encourage children to create a descriptive name for their character, such as "Mr. Silly Face" or "Ms. Fancy Face." Children can write the name of their character on the back of the bag.

3. When they are finished, invite children to put on their paper bag costumes and have a parade! Children also might enjoy a name-guessing game. Invite one child to stand in front of the class as the group describes the paper-bag face and guesses the character's name. Then have the child turn around to reveal the name they chose.

Word Play

Write the following sentence from the story on chart paper: *"Hi, cat," he said as he walked by.* Read the sentence aloud to children. Ask: *Which part of the sentence shows what Archie is saying?* Point out the quotation marks, and explain that these symbols show when a character is speaking. The words a character speaks are called *dialogue.*

Page through the book slowly with children, encouraging them to look for more sentences that contain dialogue. Write each piece of dialogue they find on the chart paper. Then invite children to read the dialogue as the characters, supplying different voices and expressions.

We All Scream for Ice Cream! (Science and Math)

Archie spends a good portion of the story with the remnants of his ice-cream cone on his face—that is, until Willie the dog happily licks it off for him! Everybody loves ice cream, and children will enjoy doing this science experiment as much as its delicious result!

Vanilla Ice Cream

4 cups crushed ice

1/2 cup rock salt

1/4 cup milk

1/4 cup heavy cream

2 tablespoons sugar

1/2 teaspoon vanilla

quart-size self-sealing bag

sandwich-size self-sealing bag

1. Help children place 2 cups of the crushed ice and 1/4 cup of the rock salt into the quart-size bag. Then have them measure and pour the milk, cream, sugar, and vanilla into the smaller bag and seal tightly.

2. Place the smaller bag inside the large bag, and show children how to squeeze the air out. Seal the outer bag and let children take turns gently squeezing it for a total of about five minutes. Encourage children to note any changes they see.

3. Next, drain the water from the larger bag and add the rest of the ice and salt. Seal as before and let children continue squeezing until the mixture in the smaller bag is thickened.

4. Remove the inner bag and cut off one bottom corner. You can serve your homemade ice cream by squeezing small portions into plastic cups. Then pass out spoons and enjoy!

Talent Show (Dramatic Play and Social Skills)

Archie loves to display his talents by putting on shows for his friends. Why not explore the talent in your classroom by putting on your own show?

◉ Invite children to recall the parts of the story in which Archie entertains his friends and name some of the things he does, such as pretending to be Peter's grandpa, putting on a giant mask, and so on. What kinds of things might children do to entertain the class? They might sing a song, do a dance, play an instrument, do a magic trick, or tell a story. Children might prefer to do their acts "solo," or team up with other classmates to perform a skit or a song. Give children time to practice their talents, and then let the show go on! Be sure to emphasize that while people may be good at doing different things, everyone has talents that make them special.

Who's at My Door? Lift-the-Flap Banner

(Language Arts, Art, and Critical Thinking)

Archie's new animal friend follows him all the way home—and although he may not know it, the cat is patiently waiting outside his door as the story ends. Invite children to invent their own tag-along animal friend for an interactive lift-the-flap banner.

1. Make copies of the banner sheet on page 32, one for each child. Provide children with scissors, glue, crayons, and sheets of construction paper. Help children cut the top and side of the door on the dotted lines to create a flap. Have children fold the door flap back, then glue the side and top edges of the page to a sheet of construction paper. (Be sure children do not glue down the door flap.)

2. Next, invite children to think of an animal they would like to have follow them home. It may be a realistic animal (such as a dog or a mouse) or a more fanciful one (such as a kangaroo or a dinosaur). Have children draw their animal friend on the construction paper behind the door flap and label the picture with the animal's name.

3. To complete the banner sheet, have children "close" the door and complete the sentences to create clues about their animal, including number of legs, what it eats, the first letter in its name, and something special it can do (such as jump, fly, or bark).

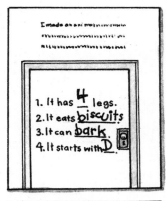

4. When children are finished, tape the sheets side by side on a wall of the classroom. Let children travel "door to door," read the clues, and guess which animal is waiting outside each one. Then have them open the door to check their guess!

Additional Resources

Cat, What Is That?
by Tony Johnston
(HarperCollins, 2001)

In rhyming verse, this book answers the question "What is a cat?" Beautiful paintings of various breeds complete this ode to the feline.

Go Home! The True Story of James the Cat
by Libby Phillips Meggs
(Albert Whitman & Co., 2000)

Children will embrace this touching and true story of a lost cat who finally finds his way into a loving new home.

Have You Seen My Cat?
by Eric Carle
(Simon & Schuster, 1987)

As a boy searches for his lost cat, he comes across a puma, a jaguar, a tiger, and several other ferocious felines before finally finding his own.

Top Cat
by Lois Ehlert
(Harcourt, 1998)

Top Cat rules the roost, until his owners bring home a new cat from the humane society. Will he learn how to welcome the new addition?

Name: _____

I made an animal friend today.
It followed me home and it's here to stay!
Read the clues from one to four.
Then guess what is outside my door!

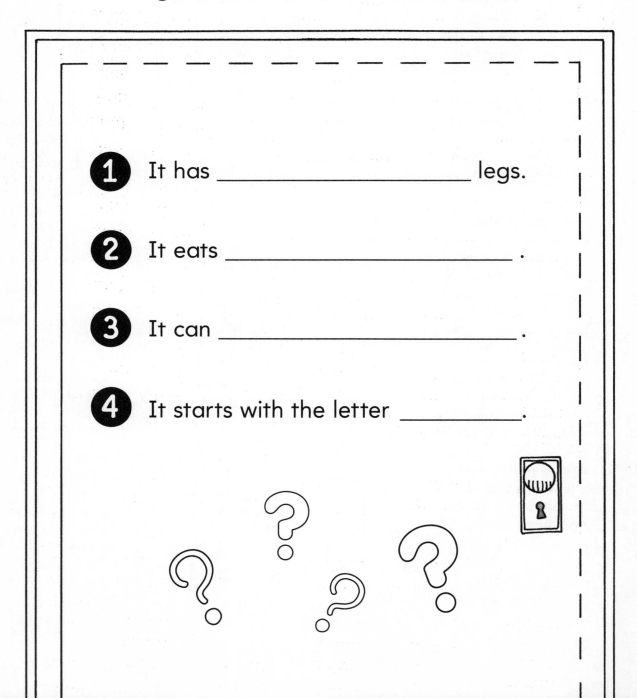

1 It has _____ legs.

2 It eats _____ .

3 It can _____ .

4 It starts with the letter _____ .

Who's at My Door? Lift-the-Flap Banner

32

Pet Show!

❖❖❖

(MACMILLAN, 1972)

When the local pet show is announced, Archie plans to enter the neighborhood cat—but when it's time to go, that cat is nowhere to be found! The show goes on, and all of his friends enter their animals and win awards. But just in time, Archie comes up with an ingenious plan to enter the contest after all. And when the cat shows up with a different neighbor, Archie's generosity lets everybody win.

Concepts and Themes

▲▲▲▲▲▲

☼ animals, pets

☼ problem-solving, ingenuity

☼ kindness, generosity

Before Reading

Begin a discussion about pets. Ask:

❋ What kinds of pets do you have at home? What kind might you like to have?

❋ What is your pet's name? How do you help take care of your pet?

❋ How do you play with your pet? What special things can your pet do?

Show children the cover of the book and read the title aloud. Tap children's prior knowledge by asking:

❋ What is a pet show? Have you ever been to a pet show? What happened there?

❋ If you were to enter your pet in a contest, what prize do you think it might win?

After Reading

Encourage children to retell the story and relate to the characters by asking:

❋ Why were all the children excited about the pet show? How do you think Archie felt when he couldn't find the cat?

❋ How did Archie manage to enter the contest without the cat? What would you have brought to the pet show if you couldn't find your pet?

Next, discuss Archie's kindness to the old woman who brought the cat. Ask:

❋ Why do you think Archie let the woman keep the blue ribbon? What would you have done if you were Archie?

❋ How might the woman have felt if Archie had taken the ribbon back? Why do you think so?

After discussing the story with children, you might share an interesting bit of trivia: The author makes an appearance as a character in the book! Show children a photo of Keats. Then page through the story and challenge children to find him. (He appears as one of the judges.)

The Best Pet Award (Dramatic Play, Language Arts, and Social Skills)

Invite children to participate in a class pet show to win their own special award.

1. In advance, invite each child to bring in his or her favorite stuffed animal from home to enter in the pet show. Make copies of the award pattern on page 37, one for every two children.

2. On the day of the show, begin by letting children have a "pet parade" around the room. Then gather children in a circle and let them take turns showing their pet to the group. Encourage children to tell their animal's name, how old it is, and why it is special to them. Children might also like to let their pets "perform" a special trick (a stuffed dog might "roll over," a stuffed parrot might "talk").

3. Next, line up all the animals and encourage children to describe them. What makes each pet special? Then invite children to become judges as well as contestants! Assign each child an animal (other than their own) to judge. Hand out the award patterns and help children cut them out. Each child gets one award. Encourage them to fill in the blanks with a superlative and the name of the animal to complete the award (for instance, *the softest cat, the prettiest bird, the quietest mouse,* and so on). Children can color the awards with crayons or markers and add glitter if they wish. Help children punch a hole in the top of the award and string with yarn to make a necklace.

4. When the awards are complete, announce the winners! Let each judge present his or her award to the recipient and hang it around the stuffed animal's neck. Celebrate by having a second parade for all the winners!

Working With Animals (Social Studies and Dramatic Play)

What is it like to have a job working with animals?

◎ If possible, arrange a trip to a veterinarian's office or to a local pet-shop. Before the trip, invite children to predict the animals and supplies they might see. Have children brainstorm a list of questions for the vet or pet shop worker, such as how they take care of the animals, what the different animals eat, how often they are fed, and so on. If a field trip is not possible, you might arrange for a veterinarian or pet-shop employee to visit the class for an interview. Then let children show what they've learned by setting up a veterinary office or a pet-shop in your dramatic play center. Include stuffed animals, empty pet-food containers, shoeboxes and blankets for "pet beds," and so on. Children can role-play taking care of the animals, feeding them, giving vaccinations, cleaning cages, and so on.

Guess That Pet! (Movement)

Invite children to learn more about their favorite pets by playing a game of charades—in reverse!

1. In advance, have children draw pictures of various pets or cut out pictures from magazines. Animals might include a dog, a cat, a fish, a bird, a frog, or a snake. Place all the pictures in a paper bag.

2. Invite one child to come forward and stand in front of the group. Pick a picture out of the bag and pin it to the child's back without letting the child see it. Have the child turn around so that the group can see the pet.

3. Next, have children in the group take turns giving the child instructions to act out the pet—but without saying the pet's name. For instance, if the secret pet is a dog, children might give instructions such as: *Walk on all fours*; *Wag your tail*; *Beg for food*; *Bark*.

4. As the child listens to the clues and follows the directions, invite him or her to guess which pet he or she has become! When the pet has been guessed correctly, the child who gave the last clue comes forward to play the next round. Continue to rotate until all the pets have been guessed and each child has had a chance to act one out.

What Do Germs Do? (Science)

Archie enters a very unusual pet in the contest—an invisible germ in a jar. Are germs really invisible? What do they do? Try this experiment to find out.

1. Gather several potatoes, peel them, and cut them into slices. Place the sliced potatoes in cold water until you are ready to do the activity. (It is best to do this experiment after outdoor time, when children's hands are dirtier!)

2. Ask children if they think they have germs on their hands. Can they see them? Pass around half of the potato slices, letting children take turns rubbing them with their hands. Place the slices in self-sealing bags, and place the bags in a shoebox labeled *Dirty*.

3. Next, have children wash their hands very thoroughly with antibacterial soap and warm water. Pass out the rest of the potato slices, again having children handle them thoroughly. Place these slices in self-sealing bags and place them in a separate shoebox labeled *Clean*. Let children look at the potatoes in each box: Can they see any difference?

4. Leave the shoeboxes in a warm, dark place for two to three days. Then open them up and compare. Children will see that the potatoes touched by dirty hands grew much more mold than those touched by clean hands. Explain that although germs may be invisible to the human eye, they are most certainly there to do their dirty work! Use the experiment to emphasize the importance of hand-washing before eating or handling food.

Word Play

Use the story to teach a mini-lesson on superlatives. Turn to the section of the book in which the prizes are awarded and read the text aloud. Write the following words on chart paper: *noisiest, handsomest, friendliest, busiest, brightest, longest, fastest, softest, slowest*. What do all the words have in common? (They all end in *-est*.)

Explain that when *-est* is added to the end of a word, it means "the most"—for instance, *friendliest* means "the most friendly," and *noisiest* means "the most noisy." (You might choose to write the root word next to each superlative on the list. Point out that words ending in *y* change spelling pattern when the *-est* is added.) Invite children to suggest more superlatives to add to the list, such as *biggest, smallest, shortest, tallest*, and so on. For additional practice using superlatives, see *The Best Pet Award* activity on page 37.

35

◆◆◆◆◆◆◆◆◆◆◆◆◆◆◆◆

Additional
Resources

✓ *Arthur's Pet Business*
by Marc Brown
(HarperCollins, 1990)

When Arthur wants a
pet of his own, he starts
a pet business to prove
he knows how to care for
animals. Both a profit
and a puppy are his
rewards!

Franklin Wants a Pet
by Paulette Bourgeois
(Scholastic, 1995)

Everyone's favorite turtle
gets a goldfish of his
own in this story about
responsibility and love.

I Want a Pet
by Lauren Child
(Tricycle, 1999)

When a young girl asks
for a variety of pets
(including a lion, a
wolf, and an octopus),
the adults in her life
point out the potential
problems—but the pet
shop owner helps her
find a solution.

The Perfect Pet
by Margie Palatini
(HarperCollins, 2003)

When Elizabeth's
parents say no to her
many requests for a pet,
she finally finds the
perfect companion in a
bug named Doug.

Pet Show Graph & Sort (Math and Science)

Use the pets featured in the story as a springboard for graphing and sorting activities.

1. First, page through the book with children and ask them to point out each animal word. (Pets in the story are as follows: *ant, mouse, cat, parrot, frog, fish, canary, dog, turtle, puppy, goldfish.*) Divide the class into small groups and assign each group one animal from the list to draw. Have children label their pictures with the animal's name.

2. To create a pet graph, attach the pictures in a horizontal row across a bulletin board or wall of the classroom. Provide children with sticky notes and have them label them with their names. Then invite children to come up to the board and attach their name under the pet they would most like to have. When the graph is complete, discuss the results. Which pet is most popular in your class? Which is least popular?

3. You can also use the pictures for sorting activities. Have children sort the pets by number of legs, skin covering (fur, scales, feathers), how the animals move (walk, fly, swim), and so on. Invite children to invent their own sorting criteria as well.

The Best Pet Award

**Best
Pet Award**

for the

_____est

____!

**Best
Pet Award**

for the

_____est

____!

Louie

◆ ◆

(GREENWILLOW, 1975)

This story introduces Louie, the shyest boy in the neighborhood. No one has ever heard Louie speak—until Susie and Roberto put on a puppet show. Louie feels an instant friendship with Gussie the puppet, and has trouble saying goodbye to her when the show is over. But when Susie and Roberto leave him a special surprise, Louie discovers that friendship is really all around him.

Concepts and Themes

▲ ▲ ▲ ▲ ▲ ▲

☼ **puppets**

☼ **feelings, shyness**

☼ **friendship**

☼ **kindness and giving**

Before Reading

Begin a discussion with children about feelings. Talk about times when children have felt happy, sad, frightened, angry, and so on. When children have had a chance to share, introduce the concept of feeling shy. Ask:

✳ What does it mean to feel shy? Have you ever felt quiet, or afraid to talk to someone new? How did it feel? What did you do?

✳ Have you ever met someone else who seemed shy, such as a child who is new in the neighborhood or at school? What are some ways you can help someone who is feeling shy? How might you make them feel more welcome?

Provide children with a few suggestions, such as saying hello, offering to share a toy or a snack, or inviting the child to play a game. Continue by asking:

✳ What are some other ways to make a new friend? What are some ways you can show your friends that you like them and care about them?

After Reading

Invite children to talk about Louie's feelings throughout the story. Ask:

✳ How did Louie feel at the beginning of the book? How did he feel when he first saw Gussie?

✳ Why do you think Louie liked the puppet so much? Why didn't he want to let go of Gussie after the show was over?

✳ How do you think Louie felt when he saw the surprise from Susie and Roberto?

Next, discuss the story from Susie and Roberto's point of view. Ask:

✳ Why did Susie and Roberto decide to give Louie the puppet?

✳ Have you ever given a friend a special surprise or a present? What was it?

✳ How did it make you feel to do something nice for your friend? How do you think it made your friend feel?

Friendship Board (Social Skills and Language Arts)

Reinforce friendship and kindness in the classroom with an interactive bulletin board display.

1. In advance, collect one photograph of each child (alternatively, children can create self-portraits). Attach children's pictures to an eye-level bulletin board and staple an envelope labeled with the child's name beneath each one. Keep a supply of note cards and pencils near the board.

2. Talk with children about ways they can show kindness and friendship in the classroom. For example, they can help a friend clean up, share a toy, play a game together, and so on. Encourage children to keep an eye out for "good deeds" in the classroom. Each time they receive kindness from a classmate, have them write or dictate the good deed on a card, sign their name, and place it in the child's envelope.

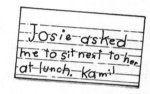

3. Encourage children to check their envelopes every few days to see the acts of friendship for which they have been recognized and thanked. You might also invite children to share the contents of their envelope with the group on a rotating basis. This is a great way to encourage kindness to others and build children's self-esteem as well!

Feelings Song (Music and Movement)

Explore emotions with children by inviting them to create their own verses to a popular song.

1. Sing the song "If You're Happy and You Know It" with children. When they are familiar with the tune and lyrics, invite children to suggest other feelings words they might use in place of *happy*, for instance: *angry, sad, surprised, excited,* and so on. What kinds of things might they do if they were feeling each way? (They might cry when they are sad, jump up and down when they are excited, and so on.)

2. Invite children to take turns inventing new verses and leading the group in a movement to match the feeling. For example:

   If you're angry and you know it, stamp your feet (stamp, stamp).
   If you're angry and you know it, stamp your feet (stamp, stamp).
   If you're angry and you know it, and you really want to show it,
   If you're angry and you know it, stamp your feet (stamp, stamp).

3. Continue to rotate until each child has had a chance to lead the group in a new verse and movement.

Word Play

Write the following quotes from the story on chart paper:

"Wow! Everybody's here! Will you please sit down?"

Read each sentence aloud to children, using an expressive voice. Ask children how they think your voice changed for each sentence. Then point out the punctuation marks. Do children know what these symbols mean? Explain that they tell the reader what a sentence should sound like: a question mark means that someone is asking a question, and an exclamation point might mean that someone is excited, surprised, or angry.

Page through the book with children, inviting them to raise their hands each time they see a question mark or an exclamation point. Have children take turns reading these sentences with the appropriate expression.

Louie's Thoughts (Language Arts)

Although Louie only speaks one word in the story (*hello*), his thoughts and feelings are portrayed vividly through his actions and the book's illustrations. Invite children to put words to Louie's thoughts with this activity.

1. Page through the book with children and help them articulate each step of the story line. Create a numbered list of story scenes on chart paper, writing a separate sentence for each. For instance:

   > **1.** Louie went to the puppet show.
   > **2.** Louie saw Gussie.
   > **3.** Louie clapped loudest when the show was over.
   > **4.** Louie had to say good-bye to Gussie.
   > **5.** Louie went home and sat in his room.
   > **6.** Louie had a dream.
   > **7.** Louie got the secret note.
   > **8.** Louie found the puppet.

2. Divide the class into small groups and assign each a different scene from the list. Provide children with large sheets of paper, pencils, and crayons and have them work together to illustrate the scene. Using the chart as a reference, have children write the story sentence at the bottom of the page. Then have them create a thought balloon for Louie and write a sentence telling what he is thinking. Children might like to use the book as a reference, studying the illustrations for clues.

3. When children are finished, bind their pages together in order and create a cover. Read the completed book aloud, inviting group members to share their pages and give reasons for their interpretations of Louie's thoughts.

Louie had to say goodbye to Gussie

Secret Surprises (Social Skills and Following Directions)

Susie and Roberto came up with an inventive way to surprise Louie: they told him to follow a long green string to find his gift. You can do the same!

◎ Invite children to practice giving and following directions as they give one another special surprises. Assign each child a secret partner and invite children to create a surprise gift, such as a drawing or a special message. Provide each child with a long string of different-colored yarn and have children hide their gifts in different spots in the classroom. Then have them use the yarn to create "trails" leading to their gifts. Have each child slip a note in his or her partner's cubby reading *Follow the long (color) string*. Then invite children to follow the directions to find their secret surprise!

Puppet Show (Art and Dramatic Play)

Children can use the patterns on page 42 to put on their own puppet show featuring Gussie and the mouse.

1. Divide the class into pairs and make one copy of the puppet patterns for each. Have children cut out the patterns and color them with crayons, markers, or paints. Children might also like to add texture with yarn, felt, fabric scraps, glitter, tissue paper, or other collage materials. Have children glue or tape their finished characters to craft sticks to make puppets.

2. Gather children together and discuss the puppet show in the book. In the story, we learn that everyone "laughed at the adventures of Gussie and the mouse," but we never learn what those adventures were. What do children think the puppet play might have been about? What did Gussie and the mouse do together?

3. After children have had a chance to brainstorm story ideas, give each pair time to rehearse their version of the puppets' adventures. Children might also like to create a simple "puppet theater" by cutting the bottom out of a large cardboard box. Set the box on its side and place it on a table for children to kneel behind. Give each pair a chance to put on a puppet show for the group.

Variation: Children can also use the puppets to enhance a reenactment of the whole story. Invite pairs of children to take turns playing the roles of Susie and Roberto as they put on their puppet show. The rest of the group can take on the roles of Louie and the other audience members. Children might even like to extend the story, telling what happens after Louie finds the puppet: Does he thank Susie and Roberto for the gift? Do they all play together? Perhaps they decide to put on another show!

Additional Resources

Clifford, We Love You
by Norman Bridwell
(Scholastic, 1990)

When the big red dog is feeling sad, his friends come to the rescue with a shower of kindness.

How Kind!
by Mary Murphy
(Candlewick, 2002)

When Hen gives Pig an egg, she starts a chain of good deeds that brings kindness to all the animals on the farm.

Poppy's Puppet
by Patricia Lee Gauch
(Henry Holt, 1999)

This fanciful story follows Poppy the puppet-maker and the magical characters he creates.

Shy Charles
by Rosemary Wells
(Penguin Putnam, 2001)

This story of a shy, quiet, but surprisingly heroic mouse shows children that timidity isn't always what it seems.

Puppet Patterns

Teaching With Favorite Ezra Jack Keats Books   Scholastic Teaching Resources

The Trip

(GREENWILLOW, 1978)

When Louie's family moves to a new neighborhood, he must leave his old friends behind. Feeling lonely on Halloween, Louie creates a city scene inside a shoebox. Reminded of his old neighborhood, he takes an imaginary trip to visit his old friends. The calls of "trick or treat" from outside his window bring Louie back from his trip—and lead him to join some new friends for Halloween night.

Before Reading

Begin a discussion with children about moving to a new neighborhood. Has anyone in the class ever had to move to a different town or start going to a new school? Ask:

✳ What did it feel like to move to a new place? Were you excited? Scared? Happy? Sad?

✳ What did it feel like to leave your old home? Did you miss your friends? How did you make new ones?

If children have not had the experience of moving, ask if they have ever met someone else who was new to their neighborhood. Ask:

✳ How do you think it feels to be the "new kid" in the neighborhood or at school?

✳ What are some ways you can welcome someone new? How can you make a newcomer feel more at home?

After Reading

Invite children to retell the story, emphasizing Louie's experiences and feelings. Guide children's retellings by asking:

✳ How did Louie feel when he moved to a new neighborhood? Do you think he was lonely? Why?

✳ How did Louie use his imagination to make himself feel better? Do you think he had fun on his make-believe trip back to his old neighborhood? What did he do there? Who did he see?

✳ What happened at the end of the story? Do you think Louie will make some new friends? What do you think the children will do together on Halloween?

Invite children to extend the story by telling about some of their own Halloween experiences. Do they like to wear costumes and go trick-or-treating? Do they think Louie will enjoy doing these things too?

Concepts and Themes

▲▲▲▲▲▲

☼ moving to a new neighborhood

☼ old friends and new friends

☼ Halloween

☼ imagination and make-believe

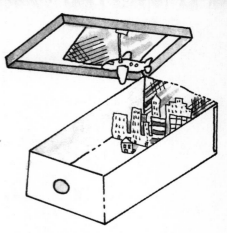

Neighborhood Dioramas
(Art and Social Studies)

Invite children to construct their own colorful neighborhood scenes. Revisit the part of the story in which Louie creates his diorama. Then have children follow the same steps, using the book as a reference.

1. Divide the class into small groups and provide each with a shoebox. Help children cut the back end off the box and cut a peephole in the front end. Then help them cut a large rectangular hole in the lid.

2. Have children paste items inside the bottom of the box to represent their own neighborhood. (If children live in different areas, they can create the neighborhood around the school.) For instance, they might create buildings from cardboard or construction paper, or build houses from small interlocking blocks. Children can also include trees, toy people, and cars. They might even like to use yarn to hang a toy plane from the box lid, just like Louie did.

3. When children have finished their neighborhood scenes, help them tape a sheet of colored cellophane over the hole in the box lid, and another sheet across the back end. (They can use two different colors if they like.) Then place the lid back on the box.

4. When the dioramas are complete, let children take turns looking through the peepholes to see all the colorful neighborhoods! How is each neighborhood alike and different?

Halloween Costume Guessing Game
(Language Arts, Art, and Critical Thinking)

At first, Louie didn't recognize his old friends with their Halloween costumes on. Help children practice descriptive skills with a Halloween costume guessing game.

1. Encourage children to think of a favorite costume they have worn on Halloween. Did they go as a princess? A pirate? A favorite story character? Have children draw a picture of themselves wearing the costume and write the name of the character beneath their illustration. On a separate sheet of paper, have children write a detailed description of the costume—but without naming their character.

2. When children are finished, display their work on a bulletin board. Post the descriptions on one side, and the pictures on the other side in mixed-up order. Let children read each costume description and guess what the child went as. Then challenge them to find the picture that matches the description and check their guess!

Paper Plane Science (Science)

In the story, Louie took an imaginary trip on a toy airplane. Invite children to explore aerodynamics by making and testing their own airplanes.

◎ Provide each child with a plain 8 1/2- by 11-inch sheet of paper, a paper clip, and a pair of scissors. Demonstrate how to construct a paper airplane as follows:

1. Fold the sheet of paper in half vertically and open it back up.

2. Fold the top corners of the sheet toward the middle line, making two triangles.

3. Fold each triangle in half toward the middle. Then fold the whole plane in half on the middle line.

4. Fold each side down to make a wing. Slide a paper clip onto the bottom of the plane.

5. Make two cuts on the back of each wing. Fold the tabs upward.

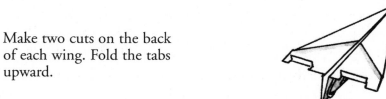

◎ Take children to an open indoor area (such as the school gym or a long hallway) to practice flying their planes. Invite them to experiment by changing the position of the tabs. How does the plane fly when both tabs are folded upward? (It soars upward in a high arc.) How about when both tabs are folded downward? (It makes a nose dive.) What might happen if children fold one tab up and the other down? (The plane will spin as it flies.) Explain that real airplanes use similar devices to lift off, touch down, change direction, and even make loops in the air!

Word Play

Write the first sentence of the story on chart paper: *Louie's family moved to a new neighborhood.* Ask children which word in the sentence tells what Louie's family did (*moved*). Page through the book and have children point out other words with *-ed* endings (*sighed, looked, pretended, wandered, stopped, turned.*) Write these words on the chart paper, using one color marker for the root word and another for the ending. Help children recognize the root of each word. Challenge them to suggest other action words for the list, then add an *-ed* ending to each (*walk–walked, play–played, jump–jumped*).

Additional Resources

Alexander, Who's Not (Do You Hear Me? I Mean It!) Going to Move
by Judith Viorst
(Atheneum, 1995)

Alexander (of *The Terrible, Horrible, No Good, Very Bad Day*) is back with a new complaint: His family is moving, and he refuses to come along. Children will relate to Alexander as he gradually learns to accept the idea of a new home.

The Leaving Morning
by Angela Johnson
(Orchard, 1992)

Through beautiful paintings and lyrical text, this tender story follows a brother and sister as they say good-bye to the familiar people and places of their neighborhood on moving day.

Trick or Treat, It's Halloween!
by Linda Lowery & Richard Keep
(Random House, 2000)

This rhyming picture book takes children through an alphabet of Halloween delights.

Trick-or-Treat on Milton Street
by Lisa Bullard
(Lerner, 2001)

Charley is sure that his first Halloween in his new neighborhood will be awful—until he goes out trick-or-treating and meets some very interesting new neighbors.

Bus	Boat	Train	Airplane	Car
✓ ✓	✓ ✓ ✓	✓	✓ ✓ ✓ ✓	✓ ✓ ✓ ✓ ✓

Travel Graph (Math and Social Studies)

Louie took an imaginary trip on an airplane. Create a transportation graph showing ways children in your class have traveled.

1. Talk with children about any trips they may have taken with their families. How did they get where they were going? Write several methods of transportation across the top of a sheet of tagboard, such as *boat, bus, train, airplane, car*, and so on. You might add a simple picture of each vehicle.

2. Have children take turns coming up to the graph and making a tick mark under each way they have traveled. (Encourage children to mark any vehicle they have been on, even if it was not for a long-distance trip.)

3. When the graph is complete, discuss the results together. Have more children traveled on a plane or in a car? How many children have traveled by train? Encourage children to discuss each method of transportation and their experiences with it. Was it fun to travel that way? Which way do children like best?

Welcome to the Neighborhood! (Language Arts, Art, and Social Studies)

Moving to a new neighborhood can be difficult. Invite children to make welcome mats to tell newcomers all about their neighborhood.

1. Talk with children about how it might feel to move to a new neighborhood. Newcomers might feel unsure because they don't know the area well. They might not know their way around the neighborhood, or know any of the people who live there. How might children make someone new to the area feel welcome? One way is to introduce him or her to the things that make the neighborhood special.

2. Provide children with sheets of colored construction paper and invite them to make neighborhood welcome mats. Encourage children to think of something they like about their neighborhood, such as the slides at the playground, the trees in the park, or the food at a particular restaurant. Have children draw a picture and add a caption, then display. You might also bind all pages together into a book, and then present it to a newcomer!

Regards to the Man in the Moon

(FOUR WINDS, 1981)

Louie is unhappy because the other children call his father "the junk man." But his father teaches him that it's not just "junk" when he helps Louie use his scraps to build the *Imagination I*. Using the power of imagination as fuel, Louie and his friends take the homemade spaceship on an adventure that's out of this world!

Before Reading

Tap children's prior knowledge about the sun, moon, stars, and space. Ask:

✳ When you look up at the sky at night, what can you see? What can you see in the sky during the day?

✳ Does the sky look different at night than it does during the day? How?

✳ If you were to fly into space on a rocket ship, what things do you think you would see on your trip?

✳ What do you think real astronauts see when they travel to space?

Show children the cover of the book and read the title aloud. Invite them to make predictions about the story by asking:

✳ What do you think the boy is riding in? Where do you think he will go?

After Reading

Help children retell key parts of the story by asking:

✳ How did Louie feel when the other children called his father "the junk man"? Do you think Louie and the other children felt differently about "junk" by the end of the story? Why or why not?

✳ Where did Louie take his friends on the *Imagination I*? What did they see?

Next, help children distinguish the fantasy elements of the book as they relate the story to their own experiences. Ask:

✳ Do you think Louie and his friends really went into space, or were they pretending? Why do you think so?

✳ When you play with your friends, do you like to make believe? What kinds of games do you play?

✳ Have you ever used your imagination to "travel" somewhere special, like Louie did? Where did you pretend to go? What kinds of adventures did you have there?

Concepts and Themes

▲ ▲ ▲ ▲ ▲ ▲

☼ recycling, finding new uses for scraps

☼ creativity, imagination

☼ the moon

☼ outer space

Word · · Play

Write the following sentence from the story on chart paper and read it aloud to children: *"Ready when you are,"* *Susie shouted.* Ask: *Which word tells how Susie's voice sounded?* (shouted). Revisit the story with children, inviting them to point out other words that describe the way characters speak. Words they might find include: *growled, yelled, gasped, whispered, cried,* and *moaned.* Invite children to take turns reading each piece of dialogue, using the descriptive word to guide their expression.

Extension Activities

Magic Junk Machine Museum
(Art and Language Arts)

Louie and his friends learned to see "junk" in a different way when they used it to build a magical spaceship. You can help children learn a similar lesson by using classroom recyclables in new and creative ways.

1. Gather a variety of recyclable materials, including empty food containers and milk cartons, Styrofoam lunch trays, shoeboxes, egg cartons, bottle caps, wood and fabric scraps, and so on. You can also include collage materials such as pipe cleaners, yarn, construction paper, and glitter. Cover a large table with newspaper and set out the materials along with glue, scissors, paints, and brushes.

2. Invite children to examine the "junk table." Where did each material come from? How might it be used in a new way? Invite children to use any combination of materials they like to build their own magical machine. Children might follow Louie's lead and build a spaceship, they might construct a special robot, or they might even come up with a completely new invention. Children can work individually or in small groups to build their machines.

3. When children are finished, display the creations in a "Magic Junk Machine Museum." Give children large index cards to use as plaques. Have them write their name, the name of their machine, and a short description of what it does. Encourage children to explore the museum and look at all the magical things that junk can do!

My Space Log (Language Arts)

Invite children to keep a journal tracking their own imaginary adventure through space!

◎ Create premade blank books of five pages each. Distribute to children and have them label each page with a day of the week, from Monday to Friday. Then invite them to imagine that they are taking a trip into outer space for one school week. Set aside time each day for children to write an entry in their logs telling what they saw and did. Did they take a walk on the moon? Explore Mars? Perhaps they even met an alien! Encourage children to use their imaginations and add pictures to go with their entries. At the end of the week, let children trade logs and share their space adventures.

Solar System Space Walk (Movement, Science, and Math)

Louie saw all sorts of "new worlds" on his trip to outer space. Introduce children to the planets and how they travel with a movement activity.

1. In advance, label ten index cards as follows: *Sun, Mercury, Venus, Earth, Mars, Jupiter, Saturn, Uranus, Neptune,* and *Pluto.* Draw a simple picture on each card. Punch two holes in the top and thread with yarn to make a necklace.

2. Choose ten children to represent the solar system and give each a necklace. Have the Sun stand in the center of the room and the planets stand in order away from the Sun (Mercury closest and Pluto furthest away). Use masking tape to mark the spot where each child is standing. Then call out "Planets Travel!" Have each planet walk around the Sun in a full circle (be sure children are moving at about the same pace).

3. When children have returned to their marks, ask which planet took the longest amount of time to travel around the Sun. Which planet completed the circle in the shortest time? Why do children think this happened?

4. Repeat the activity, letting children rotate until each has had a chance to participate. To extend children's learning, you might have the Sun hold a flashlight pointed straight ahead as the planets travel. Which planet do children think gets the most light and heat? Which planet gets the least?

Constellation Station (Science, Math, and Art)

Study stars! All you need is a few simple materials to create a stellar learning center.

1. In advance, draw simple pictures of various constellations on index cards (see right). Label each card with the constellation's name. Keep a supply of black construction paper, white crayons, and self-stick foil stars in the center. (Cut the stars apart while still attached to the backing to make counting and arranging them easier for children.)

2. Let children choose a constellation card and count out the number of stars needed, then arrange them on a sheet of black paper to match the pattern. Then have them peel off the backing and attach the stars to the paper. Children can use the white crayons to draw lines between the stars. They might also invent their own constellations.

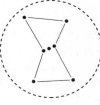

Orion

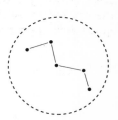

Cassiopeia

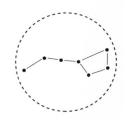

Big Dipper

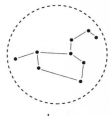

Leo

Moon Phases Wheel (Science)

Introduce children to the cyclical phases of the moon with a learning wheel.

1. Make one copy of the activity sheet on page 51 for each child. Have children cut out the wheel along the dashed lines. Then help them cut along three sides of the top wheel's window to make a flap, following the dashed lines. Show children how to place the top wheel over the bottom, insert a paper fastener through the center, and fasten in back.

2. Once children's wheels are assembled, invite them to turn the wheel to see each phase of the moon. Have children seen the moon as it looks in each picture? Have them point to the white portion of each moon. Explain that this is the part of the moon we can see because it reflects the sun's light.

3. Next, help children learn the name for each moon phase. Have children fold back the window flap and turn the wheel to see the label for each moon. Once children are familiar with the moon phases, have them fold the flap back down. Encourage children to turn the wheel, name each moon phase, and then lift the flap to check their guess.

Extension: Help children learn more about the cycles of the moon with a moon-watch calendar. (You can use your classroom calendar, or create a separate grid for moon-tracking.) Encourage children to look carefully at the moon every night. Each morning, let a child draw a picture of the previous night's moon in the calendar square for that date (you can fill in the weekend moons on Monday mornings). If it's cloudy or moonrise is after bedtime, you can consult a newspaper or almanac for information on the phase. Soon, children will begin to see a pattern in their pictures. Invite them to use what they know to predict what the moon will look like each night. You might also tell children that long ago, people used the moon's predictable patterns to keep track of time: This was called a *lunar* calendar.

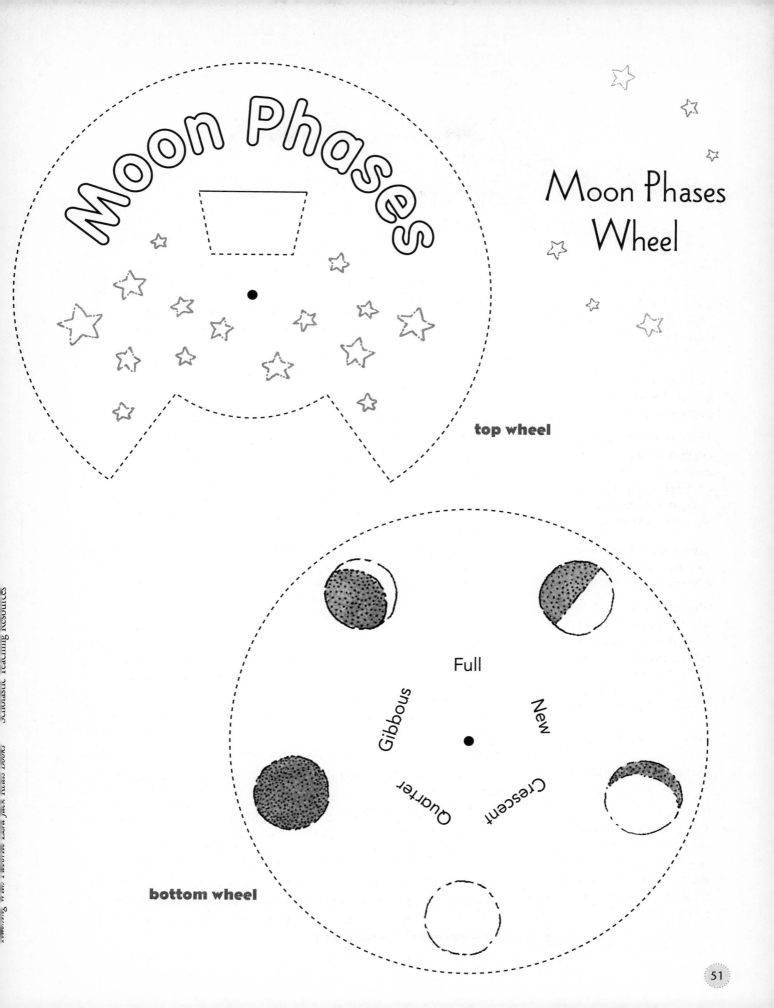

Moon Phases

Moon Phases Wheel

top wheel

Full

Gibbous

New

Quarter

Crescent

bottom wheel

Apt. 3

(MACMILLAN, 1971)

Concepts and Themes

▲▲▲▲▲▲

- ✵ apartment buildings, neighbors
- ✵ music
- ✵ senses: hearing, smell, sight
- ✵ people with special needs

When Sam hears the sad, beautiful sounds of a harmonica coming from somewhere in his apartment building, he and his brother set off to find the source of the music. They hear all kinds of noises coming from behind closed doors, until their search leads them to the dark and mysterious Apartment 3—and a special new friend.

Before Reading

Show children the cover of the book and read the title aloud. Explain that *Apt.* is an abbreviation for *apartment*. Do any children live in an apartment building, or know someone who does? If children live in different types of homes, encourage them to imagine what it would be like to live in an apartment building. Ask:

✳ How is an apartment building different from a house?

✳ Would you expect to see more apartment buildings in a city, or in the country? Why do you think so?

✳ Would you like to have many different neighbors living in the same building?

Invite children to make predictions about the story. Who might live in Apt. 3?

After Reading

Encourage children to talk about Sam and Ben's experiences in the story. Ask:

✳ Why did Sam want to find out who was playing the music? What were some of the other sounds he heard as he explored the building?

✳ How did Sam and Ben feel when they first met the man who lived in Apt. 3? Were they scared of him? Why?

✳ How did Sam and Ben's feelings change by the end of the story?

Next, encourage children to think about the story from the neighbor's point of view. Ask:

✳ How do you think the man knew so many things about the other people who lived in the building if he could not see them?

✳ Why do you think the man began to play "wild, noisy, happy" music when the boys invited him out for a walk? Do you think they will become friends?

Discuss how the characters' feelings about one another changed by the end of the story. Why is it important to get to know someone before deciding what that person is really like?

Making Music (Music and Art)

Children can make a variety of musical instruments from materials found in the classroom or at home. Let children work individually or in small groups to make one of the instruments below. Provide them with paints, crayons, and other materials to decorate their instruments. Let children take turns playing the different instruments and have a concert!

◎ **Harmonica:** Fold a small sheet of wax paper around the tooth edge of a comb and tape the edges to secure. To play, place lips lightly against the paper and hum.

◎ **Kazoo:** Cut a circle of wax paper and place over the end of a toilet-tissue tube. Smooth out the paper and secure with a rubber band. Punch holes along one side of the tube with the tip of a pencil or pen. To play, purse lips slightly and hum into the open end of the tube.

◎ **Tambourine:** Glue two heavy-duty paper plates together, facing each other. Punch holes around the edge and tie jingle bells to the plates with string or yarn. Shake to play.

◎ **Drum:** Using a pen or pencil, punch a hole in the center of the lid of an empty oatmeal container. Punch another hole through the center of the bottom of the box. Thread a long string of yarn through the holes and tie the ends together (when the drum is hung around the child's neck, it should come down to the waist). Make drumsticks by placing empty spools on the ends of two pencils and securing with glue. To play, beat the drumsticks on the box.

◎ **Shakers:** Fill empty film canisters with rice or dry beans. Secure the lid and shake to play.

◎ **Guitar:** Remove the cover from an empty shoebox. Stretch large rubber bands around the box. Glue a ruler or dowel stick to one end of the back of the box to act as the arm of the guitar. To play, strum or pluck the rubber bands.

◎ **Xylophone:** Line up several empty glass jars or bottles. Pour a different amount of water into each one. To play, gently strike the sides of the bottles with a metal spoon. Experiment with different amounts of water to create different notes. (More water creates a lower pitch; less water creates a higher pitch.)

Word Play

Sam hears many different kinds of sounds as he explores his apartment building. Revisit the story with children to find words that describe the sounds, including: *crunching, barking, crying, cheering, snoring,* and *yelling.*

Write the words on a sheet of chart paper as children point them out. Then read the list together and invite children to suggest additional sound words with *-ing* endings. Encourage them to list other sounds Sam might have heard both inside and outside his building, such as *singing, clapping, honking, beeping, clanging,* and so forth. Let children use the words to write their own noisy poem or story.

Use Your Senses! (Science and Critical Thinking)

The man in Apt. 3 knew a lot about his environment without being able to see it. Invite children to use senses other than sight to identify items in a mystery box.

1. In advance, gather items with distinctive textures and/or smells, such as a pinecone, a seashell, a lemon, an orange, a feather, a leaf, and so on. Place the items in a shoebox and close the lid.

2. Let children take turns closing their eyes or covering them with a blindfold. Remove the box lid and let children reach in and choose an item. Encourage children to handle the item and describe its texture. Is it rough? Soft? Scaly? Smooth? Does the item have a smell? Invite children to guess which item they are holding and then open their eyes or remove the blindfold to check their guess. Rotate until each child has had a chance to guess an item.

3. Use the lesson as a springboard for a discussion about people with special needs. How might someone who cannot see accomplish different tasks, such as cooking a meal, brushing their teeth, or getting dressed? How do senses other than sight help people know things about their environment?

Painting Sounds (Art and Music)

When the man in Apt. 3 plays his harmonica, Sam hears "purples and grays and rain and smoke." Music can inspire all sorts of emotions and visual images in the listener's mind.

◎ Gather a wide variety of music for children to listen to, such as classical, folk, band, and even rock 'n' roll. Be sure that you include music with a variety of tempos and moods. Provide children with paper and paints. As you play each piece, encourage children to let their imagination go to work and paint a picture. How does the music make them feel? Is it happy, sad, or lonely? Does it bring any colors or pictures to mind? For instance, a classical piece might remind children of a rainy day; a march might remind them of a parade. Children can also create abstract pictures, using colors and shapes inspired by the music's mood. Display children's paintings under the name of each genre or song. Invite them to describe their work and their feelings as they painted.

Apartment House Math

(Math and Social Studies)

An apartment building is a perfect place to explore math concepts. Provide children with paper, crayons, and pencils. Share word problems and invite children to "build" an apartment house to find the answers. Following are a few examples to try.

2 + 2 + 4 = 8

◉ The apartment building had three floors. On each floor there were four windows. How many windows were there all together?

◉ The apartment building had four floors, each with the same number of apartments. There were eight apartments all together. How many were on each floor?

◉ Twelve people lived in the building, but then three moved out. How many people were left?

You might also let children create their own number combinations and write a sentence to match. For instance, you might have them draw a three-story building with a different number of people living on each floor, then label their pictures with a number sentence (see illustration above).

Sounds Like Home (Science, Language Arts, and Social Studies)

Sam heard many different sounds coming from people's homes in his building. Invite children to tell what sounds they hear in different parts of their own homes.

1. Talk with children about the different rooms or areas they have in their homes, such as the kitchen, bathroom, family room, bedrooms, and so on. What kinds of activities take place in each room? What kinds of sounds can they hear in each?

2. Provide children with paper, crayons, and pencils. Have children divide the paper into several sections, and label each with a different room of their home. Then encourage children to close their eyes and imagine they are in each room. What sounds do they hear? Invite children to draw a picture in each section of the paper and write or dictate a caption describing the sound. For instance, children might hear the sound of the television in the family room, pots and pans clanging in the kitchen, or even the sound of a parent reading them a story in their own room.

3. Display children's work on a bulletin board for display and discussion. Which sounds are the most and least common? Which kinds of sounds are associated with particular rooms of a home?

▲▲▲▲▲▲▲▲▲▲

Additional Resources

Listen to the City
by Rachel Isadora
(Putnam, 2000)

This vibrant book celebrates the many noises of a busy day in the city, from the toot of a tugboat to the squirt of the hot dog vendor's mustard.

Max Found Two Sticks
by Brian Pinkney
(Simon & Schuster, 1994)

When two twigs fall to the ground in front of Max's stoop, he is inspired to drum out the rhythms of his city neighborhood and make music all his own.

My Building
by Robin Isabel Ahrens
(Winslow, 1998)

From the sounds of stereos to the smells of cooking, this rhyming book describes the joys of high-rise living from a child's-eye view.

Rainbow Joe and Me
by Maria Diaz Strom
(Lee & Low, 2002)

When a young artist tells her blind neighbor about the beautiful colors she creates, he shares his own way of imagining colors— with the beautiful music he plays on his saxophone.

▼▼▼▼▼▼▼▼▼▼

Jennie's Hat

◆◆

(HARPER & ROW, 1966)

Jennie's Hat
by Ezra Jack Keats

When Jennie's aunt promises to send her a new hat, she dreams of how beautiful it will be. But when the hat arrives, it is simple and plain—and Jennie is very disappointed. After her weekly trip to the park to feed the birds, Jennie wears the plain hat on an outing with her parents and looks longingly at the fancy hats all around her. But when the birds swoop down to return Jennie's kindness, she winds up with the most beautiful hat of all!

Concepts and Themes

* ☀ hats
* ☀ birds
* ☀ kindness
* ☀ nature

Before Reading

Invite children to tell what they know about hats. Ask:

* Do you ever wear a hat? What are some reasons to wear a hat? Do you wear hats to dress up, play pretend, or just to keep warm?
* Do you have a favorite hat to wear? What color is it? What does it look like? How do you feel when you wear your special hat?
* What are some different hats you know? What does a firefighter's hat look like? How about a baseball player's?

Show children the cover of the book and read the title together. Ask:

* What is Jennie wearing on her head? Why do you think she put the basket on? What might she be thinking about?

After Reading

Invite children to retell the story sequence and share their reactions by asking:

* What was Jennie waiting for at the beginning of the story? What happened when her present came? How did she feel when she saw the hat? Why?
* What do you think was the funniest thing Jennie tried to wear as a hat?
* Why did Jennie go to the park? Do you think it was nice of Jennie to feed the birds each week?
* How did the birds return Jennie's kindness? What things did they use to decorate her hat? Which item surprised you the most?
* How did Jennie feel about her hat at the end of the story? Would you like to have a hat like Jennie's?

Invite children to imagine that the birds helped them build their own "dream hats." What special items would they like the birds to include?

Make a Dream Hat (Art and Math)

The birds turned Jennie's hat into a magical creation. Invite children to make their own "dream hats" with this activity.

1. In advance, collect a hat for each child. You can buy inexpensive straw hats from a crafts store, or have children bring in an old hat from home. (Alternatively, you can have children create hats from paper plates or bowls. Simply punch a hole through two sides of the plate and attach a string of yarn to each side. Children can wear the hat by tying the yarn under their chins.)

2. Collect collage materials such as fabric strips, pom-poms, feathers, colored tissue, pieces of ribbon, old silk flowers, buttons, beads, and so on. You might also include natural materials such as pressed leaves or flowers. Invite children to glue on any combination of items they like to create a dream hat. Set aside a special time of day for children to wear their hats.

3. As an extension, help children create a Venn diagram showing how their hats are similar to and different from Jennie's. Have children list the items on Jennie's hat in one circle, the items on their own hat in the other circle, and the items on both hats in the intersection.

Bring On the Birds! (Science)

Create pinecone bird feeders to see what feathered friends you can attract.

◎ Give children dried pinecones and help them tie a string to the top end. Have them spread peanut butter over and between each layer, then roll the cone in birdseed. Hang your feeders from a nearby tree and encourage children to observe what flies by for a snack! Invite children to draw pictures of the birds they see and, if possible, find the name of each species using a field guide. Have children label their pictures and bind them together to create a special field guide for the classroom.

Word Play

Page through the book with children to find words that describe hats, including: *big, flowery, beautiful, plain, lovely,* and *wonderful.* Write these adjectives on a sheet of chart paper. Invite children to suggest additional words to describe Jennie's hat at the end of the story, such as *colorful, fancy, special, pretty,* and *unusual.* Then let children take turns describing a hat they would like to wear, and add their adjectives to the list. Use the words to create a group poem or story about a special hat.

◆ Additional Resources ◆

The 500 Hats of Bartholomew Cubbins
by Dr. Seuss
(Random House, 1976)

This delightful classic tells the story of a man who is ordered to take off his hat before the king—but each time he pulls one off, he finds another beneath it!

Hats, Hats, Hats
by Ann Morris
(HarperCollins, 1992)

Hats can tell a lot about their wearers, from what they do to where they live. Full-color photographs and a comprehensive index enhance this multicultural study.

Miss Hunnicutt's Hat
by Jeff Brumbeau
(Scholastic, 2003)

For another book that joins millinery with feathered friends, try this story about a woman who causes a commotion with her new hat—which is topped with a live chicken!

Whose Hat Is That?
by Ron Roy
(Houghton Mifflin, 1990)

This engaging concept book introduces children to 18 different kinds of hats and the people who wear them.

Who Wears It? (Social Studies and Language Arts)

Create an interactive class book about hats and the people who wear them.

1. Brainstorm a list of jobs that are associated with special hats, such as a firefighter, police officer, construction worker, chef, and so on.

2. Provide each child with a sheet of paper. Have them draw a hat on one side and the person who wears it on the other. Have children write the question *Who wears this hat?* beneath the first picture, and complete the following sentence beneath the second picture: *A _____ wears this hat.*

3. Bind children's pages together to create a book. Invite children to read the question on each page, guess the job, then turn the page to check the answer.

Jennie's Hat Story Mat (Math)

Invite children to extend the story as they practice math skills with the activity sheet on page 59. Make one copy of the sheet for each child. Have children cut out the hat pattern and paste it to a separate sheet of construction paper (they can color the hats if they wish). Then have children cut out the leaves, flowers, hearts, and fans, and have them use the pieces to act out story problems. Some examples you might try are:

◎ The birds decorated Jennie's hat with two leaves, four flowers, two hearts, and one fan. Which decoration did they use the most of? How many more hearts than leaves?

◎ The birds put four leaves, two flowers, one heart, and one fan on Jennie's hat. Then two of the leaves and one of the flowers fell off. How many items were left all together?

◎ The birds put 12 decorations on Jennie's hat. They used the same amount of each kind. How many of each?

Children can also use the hat for patterning activities. Make additional copies of the leaves, flowers, hearts, and fans. Invite children to use the cards to create a pattern across the hat brim, for instance: two flowers, one leaf, two flowers, one leaf. You might have one child begin a pattern and then pass it on to a partner to complete. Children can use crayons to incorporate colors into their patterns as well.

Jennie's Hat Story Mat

Teaching With Favorite Ezra Jack Keats Books   Scholastic Teaching Resources

CLEMENTINA'S CACTUS
EZRA JACK KEATS

Clementina's Cactus

◆◆◆

(VIKING, 1982)

Keats lets beautiful watercolor paintings tell the story in this wordless picture book. While walking near their desert home, a young girl and her father spy a small, prickly cactus plant. Clementina is fascinated by the lonely little cactus, but she must leave it behind as a thunderstorm approaches. Before night falls, the sun returns and a glorious rainbow appears. And when Clementina visits her cactus the next day, she finds it has grown a special surprise!

Concepts and Themes

▲▲▲▲▲▲

❋ **desert life**

❋ **cacti**

❋ **weather**

❋ **rainbows**

Before Reading

Find out what children already know about the desert environment. Ask:

❋ What is the weather usually like in the desert? Do you think it is mostly hot or mostly cold?

❋ What lives in the desert? Does the desert have plants? Animals? What kinds of animals might make the desert their home?

Show children the cover of the book and read the title aloud. Invite them to describe the illustration and make predictions about the story. Ask:

❋ What is a cactus? Do you see one on the cover? What does it look like? How do you think it feels to touch a cactus?

❋ Where do you think this story takes place? Why do you think so?

❋ Who might Clementina be, and what do you think she will do in the story?

After Reading

After paging through the book once to let children examine the pictures, begin again, this time letting them take turns describing the action on each page. Then invite children to retell and reflect on key events. Ask:

❋ Why did Clementina stop to look at the cactus? Why do you think it interested her so much?

❋ Why did Clementina and her father have to go home? Were you surprised to see a thunderstorm in the desert? Why or why not?

❋ What happened after the rain stopped and the sun came out? Have you ever seen a rainbow? When and where did you see it? What did it look like?

❋ Why was Clementina surprised when she went to see the cactus the next day? What did she find?

Why do you think the cactus flower bloomed when it did? Do you think the rain helped it to grow? How?

Sand Painting (Art and Social Studies)

Invite children to try out a desert art form. This technique is still used by the Navajos to create beautiful and unusual works of art.

1. Gather several empty jars or plastic containers and pour sand into each. Add powdered tempera and stir to make several different colors.

2. Provide children with heavy paper and encourage them to draw a pencil sketch for their painting. Children might like to create a desert landscape, including sand dunes, cacti, and so on. When children's sketches are complete, have them paint an even layer of glue on a small section. Then have them pour sand onto the glue using a plastic spoon. They can shake off the excess over a Styrofoam tray.

3. Have children repeat the process, continuing to work in small sections until the paper is covered. Let the sand paintings lay flat to dry, then seal them by spraying a layer of hair spray over the surface. Post children's work on a bulletin board for a beautiful desert display.

What Makes a Rainbow? (Science)

Try this experiment to create an indoor rainbow. It works best in a room with white walls.

1. Fill a smooth, wide-mouth, circular jar with water (you can also use a large plain drinking glass). Place a small mirror in the water, tilting it slightly upward.

2. Darken the room and shine a flashlight onto the mirror. Children will see a rainbow "magically" appear! (You may need to adjust the angle of the flashlight or the mirror to produce the effect.)

3. Where do children think the rainbow came from? The mirror reflects light that passes back through the water. The water bends the light, which separates it into the colors of the rainbow. Real rainbows are created by the same process: The raindrops in the air bend the sunlight and reflect the colors back. Children might be interested to know that they can only see a rainbow if the rain is in front of them and the sun is behind them.

Word Play

Revisit the story with children and ask them how it is different from other Keats books they have read. (This book has no words.) Invite children to create their own text for the book, using the illustrations and their knowledge of story structure as a guide. Let children take turns providing text for each picture as you write their narration on sticky notes. Attach the text to the pages and read your collaborative story together.

Desert Diagrams (Math, Science, Social Studies, and Language Arts)

How is the desert environment different from where children live? Use a Venn diagram to find out. (If you live in a desert region, you can compare your area to a desert in a different part of the world).

1. Before you begin, gather library books about desert regions for children to use as a reference. Then create a Venn diagram on a sheet of tagboard. Label one circle *Desert* and the other circle *Where We Live*.

2. Next, invite children to name attributes of their own environment. For instance, what is the weather usually like? What kinds of plants grow in your area? What kinds of animals live there? Help children research the same aspects of the desert environment. As children gather information, write facts that apply only to the desert in the first circle, those that apply only to your area in the second circle, and facts that apply to both areas in the intersection. You can incorporate social studies by choosing a particular desert and researching how the people there live, such as what kinds of clothing they wear and what kinds of homes they live in. Have children use the diagram to compare life in the desert with life in your area.

3. To conclude, invite children to imagine that they lived in the desert. What things would be different? What would stay the same? Encourage children to draw a picture of themselves in a desert environment and write a few sentences describing an aspect of their desert life.

Desert Blooms (Art and Science)

After the rain, Clementina was surprised to see a beautiful flower on her cactus. Children can use water to "grow" their own desert blooms with this activity.

1. Set up a work station with plain white basket-style coffee filters, several different colors of food coloring, plastic cups, pipe cleaners, and a pitcher of water.

2. Have children put drops of food coloring on different spots of a dry coffee filter. Next, help them pour a small amount of water into a plastic cup. Have children place the coffee filter inside the cup so that the flat bottom is just touching the water. What happens to the filter? (The water travels up the filter and causes the colors to spread.) Let children create several different "flowers," trying out different color combinations and patterns.

3. Lay the coffee filters out to dry. Then show children how to pinch the bottom and fan out the edges of the filter to create a flower shape. Help children attach pipe cleaners to their flowers to create stems. Gather groups of flowers and place them in clear plastic jars. You can place your desert bouquets in various spots to brighten up your classroom, rain or shine!

Caring for Cacti (Science)

Plant a mini-desert in your classroom!

1. Gather a variety of small cacti. These can be purchased very inexpensively at a gardening center. Depending on the time of year, you may want to include flowering cacti (for instance, the prickly pear cactus blooms in spring and summer). You will also need sandy potting mix, gravel or crushed stones, and a large, wide-mouth glass container (such as an aquarium).

2. Have children put on rubber gloves before they begin planting to protect their hands from getting pricked. Help them pour a layer of the sandy soil on the bottom of the container and place the cacti on top. Then, using a large spoon, have them place more soil around each plant. Cover the top of the soil with a layer of gravel.

3. Place the cactus garden in a fairly sunny spot (direct sunlight is unnecessary) and water it very infrequently—remember, too much water can cause a cactus to die. Invite children to observe their garden on a regular basis and watch for any changes.

4. To extend children's learning, you may want to grow a woodland plant in the classroom as well. Encourage children to note the differences between the two types of plants and what they need to thrive (woodland plants need much more water). To illustrate the reason behind this, try placing one plastic bag over a stem or the top of a cactus, and another plastic bag over a leaf of the woodland plant. Tie each bag closed with a string and leave the plants in a sunny spot for one day. Then check to see which bag has the most water droplets. Why do children think the woodland plant lost more water than the cactus? Explain that cacti must conserve water to survive in the desert environment.

Additional Resources

Alejandro's Gift
by Richard E. Albert
(Chronicle, 1996)

Lonely in his remote desert dwelling, Alejandro builds an oasis to attract his animal neighbors.

Cactus Hotel
by Brenda Z. Guiberson
(Henry Holt, 1993)

This book takes children through the life cycle of the giant saguaro cactus and introduces the many animals that call it home.

The Desert Alphabet Book
by Jerry Pallotta
(Charlesbridge, 1994)

Lead children on an alphabetical tour of the plants, animals, and natural phenomena that make up the desert environment.

Way Out in the Desert
by T. J. Marsh & Jennifer Ward
(Northland, 1998)

In this charming spin on "Over in the Meadow," children count along with the creatures of the Sonoran Desert. A glossary of plants and animals appends this fun and informative book.

An Ezra Jack Keats Celebration: Culminating Activities

Use the following activities to wrap up your study of Ezra Jack Keats and celebrate children's learning.

Classroom City

Invite children to show what they've learned about the urban environments of Keats's stories by building their own city right in the classroom. Provide children with materials such as unit blocks, interlocking blocks, empty milk cartons, paints, and construction paper. Children can paint milk cartons or other empty food containers to look like tall buildings. They can build shops and other structures from blocks. Encourage children to include elements they've seen in Keats's stories, such as sidewalks, traffic lights, mailboxes, and so on. Children might also like to add construction-paper trees, toy people, and small cars to their minicity. When the city is complete, invite another class over for a tour.

Skyline Mural

Invite children to create a skyline mural to decorate a wall of your classroom. You might show children photographs of city skylines (such as New York or Chicago) before they begin. Then lay a large sheet of craft paper on the floor and have small groups work on different sections of the skyline. Encourage them to paint a variety of different-shaped buildings, birds, clouds, and a sun shining high above the city. When dry, hang the mural on a wall and use it as a backdrop for children's performances (see miniplays activity).

Character Charades & Miniplays

Invite children to take on the roles of different Keats characters for a guessing game. Place character names in a paper bag. Let children take turns picking a character and telling facts about themselves without using their name, for example: *I built a spaceship and took an imaginary trip to the moon* (Louie). *I came to Peter's birthday party with my pet parrot* (Amy). Invite the group to call out their guesses, and rotate until each character has been guessed correctly.

Children can also take on the roles of characters to put on miniplays of their favorite stories. Divide the class into small groups and assign each a story to act out. Give children time to study the book and invent their own dialogue for the characters. Children can use simple props and costumes to add to their performances, such as a chair and a baby doll for *Peter's Chair* or rain hats and boots for *A Letter to Amy*. When children have had time to rehearse, let them take turns putting on their shows for the rest of the group.

Vote on It!

Invite children to vote for their favorite Keats stories and tally the results. Write the titles children have read across the top of a sheet of tagboard. Provide each child with an index card labeled with their name and have them attach the card beneath their favorite story. As you discuss the results, invite children to tell the reasons behind their votes. Why was the story they chose special to them?